May God bless you Margaret
now and always.

J. P. Wilkinson

About the Author

This is the author's first book; in which she writes about her extensive cycle journeys all over the world. It has been a wonderful adventure to have cycled in so many countries; and the author hopes it will inspire others to pursue their dreams as she did.

I would like to dedicate this book to my husband, John, who has been a staunch companion on all the cycle tours described in this book. Without him I might never have ventured so far afield, let alone cycled; and this book would not have been written.

J. P. Wilkinson

Around The World On A Bicycle

AUSTIN MACAULEY
PUBLISHERS LTD.

A CIP catalogue record for this title is available from the British Library.

ISBN 9781785549731 (Paperback)
ISBN 9781785549748 (Hardback)
ISBN 9781785549755 (EBook)

www.austinmacauley.com

First Published (2016)
Austin Macauley Publishers Ltd.
25 Canada Square
Canary Wharf
London
E14 5LQ

Acknowledgments

I would like to thank everyone who has contributed towards my writing this book, in particular: -

The Wigan Library staff, for all their help and encouragement:
They have patiently taught me how to use a word processor over the past year. Without them I would not have been able to make the necessary preparations I needed to write this book.

Friends, at home and abroad, members of St. James' Church and the staff and pupils of St. James' C.E. Primary School, Wigan:
They have faithfully prayed for us each time we have travelled. Their prayers have sustained us on all our journeys; and for these we have been, indeed, most grateful.

Our Christian brothers and sisters overseas who have provided us with accommodation during our travels:

Special mention must be given here to Ming Seong and his wife Catherine in Singapore, for all their help and support.
David, our friend and travel consultant:
David has arranged and booked all the flights we have taken for our cycle tours.

Paul Hewitt Cycles, Leyland, Lancashire:
Since 2000 Paul and his staff have maintained and serviced our bicycles, which we purchased from him in 1999 and

2005. Their support and encouragement has been invaluable.

My husband, John:
John has encouraged and supported me throughout. Without his inspiration I would not have been able to write at all.

Contents

Foreword

In 1992, at the age of 51, my husband, John took early retirement, from H. J. Heinz Ltd., where he had worked as a fork-lift truck driver and food processor for nearly 25 years.

On coming home one evening, shortly before he finished, he told me that one of his workmates had asked him what he proposed to do with his free time when he left full time employment, to which John replied that he was going to cycle round the world with his wife!

How true this was! But neither of us thought that one day we would, indeed cycle on every continent in the world (with the exception of Antarctica!). It was certainly a dream I had had for a long time, since 1984 when I did my first solo cycle tour in Ireland. I had always hoped I would find someone with whom I could share such a journey. And, to be quite honest, I didn't think it would be advisable for me to cycle as a woman on my own, especially in countries with a different culture from ours. I hadn't shared this with John yet; so I was, naturally delighted when John told me what he had said.

My cycle touring started in 1960 at the age of 15, when I spent a weekend cycling in Surrey, with a friend, staying in youth hostels. I was still at school at the time and had ridden a bicycle since I was 5 years old. I used my bike to go to school, to do my paper round and for the pure enjoyment of cycling. I have continued cycling as a general means of transport, ever since.

I did some more touring during the summer holidays, the year I left School, in 1961. This time I spent two weeks cycling and youth hostelling in Sussex and Kent, with a friend from swimming club. The next time I was to do any cycling touring was in 1984, in Ireland, at the age of 39! For the first time, I owned a "decent" bicycle with a set of Derailleur gears, drop-handle bars and even a cross bar! With a more efficient bike, I was now able to discover what potential there was in long-distance cycling.

By now I was "hooked" and spent most of my holidays from working full-time cycling throughout Britain, visiting Scotland, Wales and Ireland (for the second time) and France twice. I did all these journeys alone, staying in youth hostels, or camping in my small tent.

In 1988 I went with four friends (two men and another woman) to cycle in Tunisia. This was my first experience of cycling outside Europe and in a completely different culture; we took our bikes on the plane from Gatwick Airport and flew to Tunisia. I was now confident to do such a trip, by plane, alone; so the following year I flew to Nice and spent two weeks cycling and camping in the French Alps!

In 1990 I met John on a walking holiday in North Wales; and we married the following year.

I left my home in London and came to live in Wigan. But first I did my last cycling tour alone! I took the ferry from Portsmouth to St. Malo, in France and cycled in Brittany for two weeks. This must have inspired John, for, while we were still "courting" and he was visiting me in London, John decided to buy a touring bike! He then started to cycle regularly, after a break of over twenty years!

Our first cycle tour together was in October, 1991, when we spent ten days travelling with a small tent, through the Jura Mountains on the Swiss- French Border, from Geneva to Grenoble and back again. By now John was as enthusiastic as me!

However, we did not venture out of Europe until 2004, when we went to New Zealand to cycle for six weeks. Then we continued to cycle around the world for the next nine years and, at the same time, raised several thousand pounds for various charities, including two of our local parish churches.

We are very grateful to all those who have sponsored us over the years. It has encouraged us to keep going when the times were tough; especially as so many have prayed faithfully for us every time we travelled.

We have always paid our own way for everything, including the airfare (the most expensive), food and accommodation. The exceptions, for the latter, have been when we have received hospitality from the Christians we have met on our travels. Whenever we are able we will give donations to the work they are doing for the Lord, in their own country; and, of course, we pray for them and keep in touch with as many as we can, either by e-mail or handwritten letters.

We have always arranged our own trips (apart from the flights); and we depend entirely on the Lord to supply all our needs each time we venture somewhere new. Our faith has been tremendously rewarded and we have both been very blessed.

I have written many articles over the years for our churches' magazines; and, as a result several people have encouraged me to write a book on our adventures. We have been invited to give talks to various church groups and our local primary school; and we have found this to be a very rewarding experience.

My husband John has been, without a doubt, the source of most of my encouragement, especially as he has taken over so many of the domestic "chores" to give me more freedom to write!

This book describes our cycling adventures outside of Europe. It will require another to include those nearer home!

Chapter One

New Zealand: 2004

Part One: Wigan to Singapore

Very early in the morning on 2nd November, 2004 we set off on our bikes to cycle to Manchester Airport in order to take the 10am flight to Singapore. Our feelings were those of apprehension, mixed with excitement and anticipation of a great adventure. The important thing was to take one step at a time and endeavour to keep our eyes firmly fixed upon Our Lord Jesus. This was to be our salutary reminder throughout the next seven weeks.

We had a very comfortable, although tiring, flight to Singapore. The crew, mostly Chinese, were very helpful and courteous, we thoroughly enjoyed the oriental cuisine and a wide range of drinks – both alcoholic and otherwise! On our arrival in Singapore, on 3rd November, we were greeted by a warm, hospitable climate, the lovely people we met and the tropical weather. A Malay staff member at the airport advised us about cheap accommodation and showed a keen interest in our bikes, as well as our forthcoming tour. We took her advice and cycled 13 miles to the Geylang

Road district, not far from the city centre. On our way we were delighted to see a Christian church with the scripture verse: "Jesus said, I am the Way, the Truth and the Life" (John 14: 6), written in both English and Chinese, across what was a very undistinguished building. This church was in the Malay, and therefore predominantly Muslim, district of Singapore. It really did uplift our "jet-lagged "spirits! Little did we know that in just over 6 weeks, we would be worshipping there and experiencing some wonderful Christian fellowship.

After passing by very ornate Buddhist temples and mosques, loads of people and traffic, we found a hotel which was cheap, clean and run by a delightful Chinese family who had never had cyclists (nor possibly even Westerners) stay there before. It was a Chinese bank manager who came out of his office when he saw us, a bit lost and bewildered, looking for somewhere to stay, and guided us to the "Meng Yew Hotel". This was truly an answer to prayer!

We stayed in Singapore for two nights and had two and a half days in which to explore this magical place before flying to Christchurch in New Zealand. It was a great experience; we were the only Europeans in a district populated by three major ethnic groups – Malay, Chinese and Indian. The Malays and Tamil Indians are nearly all Muslims, the remaining Indians being Hindus and Sikhs and the Chinese either Buddhist or Christian.

The Chinese who are Christian are among the most devoted and committed we have ever met. Praise the Lord for their marvellous witness in Singapore!

It was good to see how these three diverse groups live together with mutual respect, in relative peace and harmony. Whilst we were there "Diwali" (a Hindu festival) and "Ramadan" (a Muslim festival) were being celebrated in districts just a few miles from each other. The "Malay village", where Ramadan was being celebrated, was near where we were staying; so at night, when the fast was over, there were scores of people, including us, tucking into some of the nicest food we have ever tasted!

We were able to cycle round Singapore City fairly easily and see some of the famous sights, as well as swim in the South China Sea from the nearby beach. It was warmer than Wigan Baths! We also ate some exquisite Chinese and Indian food at the nearby street cafes, with the local people.

Whilst in Singapore we experienced our first monsoon: Jan was swimming in the sea at the time, quite unperturbed! However, as the lightning approached closer it was time to find shelter, of which there were several along the sea front. As we sheltered from the storm we were joined by two young Chinese teenagers – a boy and a girl aged about sixteen. As we introduced ourselves to one another and started to chat, we discovered we were all Christians! It was a delight to have met Priscilla and Neil, who gave us their e-mail addresses and asked us to keep in touch. We passed these on to the young people at St. Mark's Church when we got back to Wigan; so they could establish a link between the Youth Clubs at each Church.

We left Singapore on Friday 5th November, in the evening, knowing we would be back again and thoroughly looking forward to returning in six weeks' time. Another adventure was about to begin!

Part Two: From Christchurch to Greta Valley

At 9.05pm we took a flight to Christchurch on New Zealand's South Island, arriving there the next day at 10:30am, somewhat jet-lagged. However, as we left the airport and started cycling towards the city centre the fresh spring breezes soon woke us up.

Our first impression of New Zealand was as if we had been in a "time-machine" which had fast- forwarded us from November to May! The birds were singing, spring blossoms and flowers abounded and the trees were fresh and green. It was quite amazing – almost like being in England during spring. We felt very strange at first, as we couldn't have been further away, the next stop, literally, being Antarctica! We were certainly a long way from home!

Once we arrived in the city centre of Christchurch, just six miles from the airport, we soon found the youth hostel, having enquired with the local tram driver as to its whereabouts. Yes, they still have trams - just like there used to be in Wigan and London when we were children during the 1950s.

We stayed at the youth hostel for the weekend, which gave us time to recover from our jet lag and explore this lovely city. We also enjoyed meeting people, of all ages, from many parts of the world, who were far away from home and travelling independently, just like us. Over the next few weeks we made new friends; and always experienced a genuine "camaraderie" at all the youth hostels we stayed in.

Christchurch is very reminiscent of Oxford and has an English "feel" about it and yet it is quite cosmopolitan at the same time. Were able to attend Christchurch Cathedral where they were celebrating 100 years since its inception, in conjunction with Christchurch College (its namesake) in Oxford, where they were commemorating 1000 years! The morning service was a "Sung Eucharist," to which many dignitaries had been invited, including several Maori, of which one was the Bishop himself. The cathedral was packed full and, after the service, sherry and delicious chocolate cake were served.

In the evening a very different service was held at the cathedral: this time it was an informal jazz service, again packed full of mainly young people, many of whom were either Maori or South East Asian. It was a very joyful occasion in which we were invited to get up and dance. In the end we couldn't resist any longer and as we started dancing we were soon joined by a host of the young people and a good time was had by all.

On Monday 8th November, in the morning, we set off to begin our epic bike ride through New Zealand, heading north along the east coast of South Island, towards Picton, where we planned to take the ferry over to North Island. As we started cycling, we realised there was a problem with the gear change on Jan's bike; so we went straight to a bike shop in the city centre. At first it was thought to be a slack cable which was causing the problem, but, on closer inspection by the bike mechanic, it was discovered that the outer casing of the cable had worn and the wires inside had frayed and were almost ready to snap! We really did praise God and thank Him for His timely intervention! Towns, let alone bike shops, are few and far between in New Zealand.

On this, our first full day of "proper cycling" we managed to travel just over fifty miles, for which we were very pleased, having had a late start on our journey. Our route took us through some lovely countryside, which reminded us very much of England. It was a warm, sunny day and the terrain became hillier the further north we travelled. As we passed through the small towns, of which there were very few, it was evident we were not in England and, what are called villages we would describe as "hamlets".

New Zealand is roughly the same size as Great Britain, but has a population of only 4 million. There are probably more sheep than people! However, the folk we did meet were very friendly indeed and always willing to help in any way they could. Their friendliness and hospitality reminded us very much of our experience of cycling and travelling in Ireland. Interestingly, both countries are sparsely populated, a factor, no doubt, which contributes to the genuine welcome we've received in both these countries.

Our first stop was in a place called "Greta Valley," which was a very small village. Here we were able to pitch our tent and camp overnight on a local farm. The owners even allowed us to use their kitchen to prepare our tea that evening and our breakfast the following morning, trusting us to lock up when we left, as everyone had gone out for the day, either to school, which was 30 miles away, or for shopping 50 miles away! We appreciated, very much, the manner in which they trusted us.

After 4 nights of not sleeping very well in "proper" beds, we had our best night's sleep, since leaving home, in our small tent. Thus, we were refreshed to continue our journey onwards.

Part Three: From Greta Valley to Rotorua

We left Greta Valley, on New Zealand's South Island, on Tuesday, 9th November and headed along the east coast towards Picton, where we would take the ferry to Wellington, on the North Island. This was a two-day journey which took us through some very spectacular scenery, consisting of hills, becoming steeper, two mountain ranges and a beautiful, rugged coastline, populated with seal colonies. We saw very few people, plenty of sheep and the miles between the small towns were numerous.

Over the next few days we experienced warm, sunny weather with clear, blue skies; so, despite the hard work cycling uphill, we had some magnificent views – all worth the effort! This was one of New Zealand's busiest roads as it went to the ferry which linked the two islands. There were, therefore, several heavy goods vehicles, nearly all attached to trailers carrying sheep; and these travelled at break-neck speed with very little warning to us cyclists. We were exceedingly grateful for the prayers of our friends back home. They were certainly answered, as we were kept safe in spite of these hazards which gave us some scary moments.

Arriving at Picton we pitched our tent; and the following morning we enjoyed a refreshing swim in the sea, which was as cold as it is in England during our summer! Our journey across the Marlborough Straits, from South to North Island, gave us a well-earned rest and we were able to relax in the sun for a few hours.

Wellington, the capital of New Zealand, is a truly beautiful city. It is very modern, but surrounded by mountains and a clear, blue sky, it is a picture to behold. We stayed in the youth hostel there, which was purpose-built and very well equipped. Here we were able to cook some "proper" meals with provisions bought from a nearby supermarket. When cycling we had to rely on food we could easily carry. This consisted of mainly bread, cake, fruit, jam, peanut butter, honey and cheese. The food in New Zealand is very good and a lot cheaper than in England. The Lord really did supply all our needs: our money went a long way and we were always provided with shops, just in time before our stocks got too low. Food for cyclists is as essential as petrol is for a car!

We continued our journey from Wellington, northward along the Kapiti coast as far as Poyaparam, where we stayed with Pamela and David whom we had met in England at Siloth, near Carlisle, where we were all on holiday in our camper vans. We didn't think we would see them again; and here we were enjoying very kind hospitality in their lovely home in New Zealand! They really did look after us and sent us on our way very refreshed and replenished.

Over the next three days we cycled through some very varied scenery and some extreme weather conditions, to Rotorua where we planned to visit Jan's cousin, whom she'd not seen for 36 years. We stayed in a motel the first night, at the end of a very cold, wet day, where we were grateful for the warmth and shelter it provided. At the end of the next day there was no available accommodation; both the hotels were full, there was no campsite and we were high up in the mountains, where it was too cold to pitch our tent and use our lightweight summer sleeping bags. However, the Lord answered our urgent prayers and we spent the night at a nearby army training camp, in the barracks. We saw the sergeant in charge and we told him we were doing a sponsored bike ride for our friend Katie, to raise money for her to do voluntary missionary work in Brazil. He, literally, "pulled out all the stops" and shelter was provided. Accommodation may have been spartan, but for us it was sheer luxury: There were clean white sheets, as many thick grey blankets as we required, an old-fashioned six-foot bath, in which we could have a long, hot soak and a boiler, so we could have a brew!

We left the army camp the next day at 8am and were greeted by very cold, wet and windy weather. After stocking up with a few provisions we continued our journey, cycling up through the mountains over the "Desert Road", so-called because there is absolutely nothing for the next 40 miles! As we reached the summit, miraculously the skies cleared, the sun came out and we were able to see the spectacular sight of the snow-clad "Ngauruhoe" – North Island's highest mountain.

Our route took us on to Lake Taupo, the largest in New Zealand. It looked just like the sea and we camped overnight, not far from its shores. The next day we arrived at Rotorua, a beautiful city in the middle of a large area of geo-thermal landscape, where there are many hot springs, emitting some unusual smells – rather like rotten eggs! However, we soon got used to it.

We spent two days in Rotorua where we had a very happy reunion with Jan's cousin Tommy and his wife Carazon, who is from the Philippines. The years just slipped away, there was plenty to talk about and we all got on famously together.

Reluctantly, we parted company and set off for the next stage of our adventure, looking forward to exploring more of the South Island. Hence we took the coach back to Wellington in order to have more time to do this. Our bikes safely stored in the boot, we retraced the several hundred miles we had cycled and it was hard to believe we had come so far! We certainly felt we had earned this day's rest.

Part Four: From Wellington to Christchurch

On Monday, 22nd November 2004, on a clear, sunny day we took the ferry from Wellington, on the North Island, to Picton on the South Island. Here we camped overnight; and the next day cycled 81 miles, from the east coast to St. Arnand, high up in the mountains, en route to the west coast. The weather deteriorated, becoming very cold and wet; thus we arrived at St. Arnand Youth Hostel soaked to the skin! However, praise be to God, we were provided with a small two-bunk room, equipped with a heater, where we were able to warm up and dry out!

The following day there was fresh snow on the mountains and it was cold and crisp as we cycled through towards Inangahna, 70 miles away. This route took us through mountains, overlooking deep river gorges. The scenery was spectacular, as were the views we had from the several summits we climbed. We spent the night at a backpackers' hostel where we relished in the luxury of a log fire by which we ate our bread and cheese followed by hot chocolate, an early night and a good sleep.

We continued to Westport where we stayed at the youth hostel for two nights and had a "rest day". This gave us the opportunity to do some washing and explore some of the rugged west coast of the South Island. It rains a lot there but on this day it was sunny and dry, although very windy. During our walk we popped into a small church where a young man was practising on the piano and he gave us an impromptu recital of our favourite hymns and Christian songs. It was very refreshing to enjoy such fellowship together.

Our journey took us further south, along the west coast for several hundred miles, over three mountain passes, each of which climbed 5, 8 and 10 miles; and through two glacial regions. It was very cold at times and also quite wet. However, the hard, uphill cycling kept us warm, we always had sufficient food to give us energy and we were provided with shelter each night. We either slept in our tent or stayed in youth hostels or backpacker hostels. We didn't have much problem sleeping even though our tent leaked badly on one occasion, when it rained heavily all night!

One of our "rest days" was spent at Okavito in New Zealand's smallest youth hostel, which had been converted from a 19th Century school house in 1960, (incidentally, the year Jan started youth hostelling at the age of 15!). There were only nine bunks, situated in two rooms, one of which served as a kitchen-cum-living room; and there was just one outside toilet. The atmosphere here was great; and on the day we left we were all reluctant to part company, as we had got to know each other so well.

At Okavito we did two fantastic walks – one along the coast and lagoon and another to the top of the mountain, which formed the backdrop of the village. The scenery here was such as we'd never experienced before and peculiar only to New Zealand. It was beautiful, but the best was yet to come!

We finally left the west coast at Haast. From here we headed east as far as Wanaka, where there is a large lake (in which we both had a swim), surrounded by snow-capped mountains. This journey included cycling over Haast Pass – one of the most horrendous rides we have ever experienced!

There were hairpin bends and strong winds, which came from our right at each bend and nearly blew us off our bikes! In order not to be blown over the edge we had to keep in the middle of the road and pray that nothing was coming towards us from round the bend! It was a miracle we were able to stay on our bikes and, it was during this time that we concentrated all our effort on praying, especially for Katie. Thus, we were given the courage to persevere. When we reached the top John was, literally blown off his bike by a sudden gust of wind! Mercifully, there was a barricade on the roadside (previously these were non-existent) and no harm was done. We certainly didn't need to do bungee jumps (for which New Zealand is famous) to get the adrenaline going!

Despite potential dangers and a serious mechanical problem with John's bike (discovered two miles from Wanaka where it was fixed, after two days waiting for the part to be delivered from Christchurch), The Lord certainly protected us and we were kept safe.

On 9th December Jan celebrated her 60th Birthday, cycling over a mountain pass with a climb of more than 3000 feet. She praised God for the strength to do 70 miles on a day she'll never forget!

The next day we arrived at Lake Tekapo – a glacial lake the colour of turquoise, surrounded by snow-capped mountains. We spent three nights, camping in our small tent, in the youth hostel grounds situated on the lakeside. At night it was freezing; we woke up each morning to find ice on our tent door and frost on the ground! During the day it was sunny and warm and shorts and T-shirts sufficed; but at night we needed extra duvets, provided by the youth hostel warden, to keep us warm.

Jan had a swim in Lake Tekapo, in water which was 4°C (37°F) and found it very invigorating! We also climbed "Mount John" and experienced some of the most beautiful scenery we have ever seen.

Both Wanaka and Lake Tekapo and the journeys in between were the highlights of our holiday. We also experienced spiritual refreshment in each of these places: At Wanaka we went to the mid-week Holy Communion at a nearby Church and were very blessed by the fellowship we had. Then at Lake Tekapo we attended a Christmas Carol Service, in which the local children performed the Nativity in the "Church of the Good Shepherd" – the smallest in New Zealand. Again, we were very blessed with sweet fellowship as we prayed and worshipped with our brothers and sisters in Christ. In each of these churches there was a clear window behind the altar, through which the lake could be seen, surrounded by the snow-capped mountains. No stained-glass windows needed here!

Reluctantly we left Lake Tekapo and cycled for two days to Christchurch, covering over 140 miles. There we were able to relax for a few days, exploring this lovely city and cycling around the scenic coastal and mountainous region of the Banks Peninsular, situated on the east coast.

Unfortunately, in 2010 an earthquake destroyed a good bit of Christchurch, including its beautiful cathedral. But we have heard, from a recent visitor, that it has now been restored to its former glory.

We were particularly blessed when we attended midday Holy Communion Service, conducted in Maori, at the cathedral, after which we all enjoyed an Indian meal at a nearby restaurant. It was good to have such fellowship with the Maori Christians and share the joy of Christmas. After six weeks of cycling in New Zealand, on Saturday, 18th December we flew to Singapore with many happy memories, which we will treasure for the rest of our lives.

Finale: From Singapore to Wigan

We left New Zealand on a cold, wet windy day and arrived in the tropical warmth of Singapore at 7.30pm on Saturday, 18th December. Our journey from the airport to the Chinese-owned hotel where we had previously stayed, in the Geylang Road district, on the outskirts of Singapore City, was about 20 miles along the scenic East Coast Park. Here we experienced a completely different culture to the one we had left behind in New Zealand. There were more people for a start; and these consisted of mainly Chinese and Malay families celebrating the weekend with numerous barbeques along the sea front. The atmosphere was warm and colourful, with inviting aromas exuding from exotic food being cooked. We resisted the temptation to stop and mingle with these friendly people and continued to cycle, arriving at our hotel at 9.30pm., where we were warmly greeted by the owners who remembered us well.

Singapore is a great place and we really had looked forward to returning and being able to spend some more time there, in particular going to worship at the church we had seen on our first visit. It was a lot easier to settle this time as we were familiar with our surroundings. We knew which shops to go to for the food we required, where to eat out and we were very much "at home" in the "Meng Yew" hotel. The climate was welcome too: It was good to shed a few layers of clothing and wear our shorts and T-shirts again. And this time we were able to work the air-conditioning – a great asset!

The following day, after a refreshing night's sleep in a clean, comfortable bed, we set out to cycle to the Chinese Christian Church about two miles along the main road. We couldn't remember the exact time of the service; so we arrived early, just before 10am. Only to discover the main service started at 10.50am. However, the place was full of children and young people who had been attending Sunday school and Bible classes. They were very friendly towards us and extremely polite. There were several adults, mostly teachers and youth leaders, as well as the pastor, who all made us very welcome.

We were given locks and keys for our bikes and then, having secured these, we were invited to join the church "staff" for breakfast! This was a virtual feast, more like a banquet with plenty of home-cooked, delicious Chinese food. The Chinese love their food so we were in good company! We didn't have any problem in accepting their generous offer to sample all the various dishes and, having satisfied our genuine hunger, we were invited to join the service of worship.

This was, indeed a wonderful experience. There was such joy expressed in the singing and the songs were easy for us to follow – some we knew and others we didn't. The time of prayer was so inspiring and we were prayed for over and over again! The warmth of their Christian love for us was truly amazing. This was something we will never forget and even writing about it now brings great joy; we were really very richly blessed on that day.

When the service of worship, which lasted over an hour and included a powerful sermon, was over, it was followed by another service of "Breaking of Bread," to which we were warmly invited. This lasted another hour! However, the time just flew by and we felt as if we could have stayed with these dear folk praising our Lord all day!

The first service was conducted in English, and then the sermon was interpreted in Chinese for those who didn't speak English. The second service was in Chinese and we wore earphones in order to receive the English translation. After two hours of worship we were invited to share yet another meal with our Chinese friends. This was even more sumptuous than our breakfast; and more enjoyable was the time of fellowship we had together. One lady, Elizabeth, a retired nurse, gave us her address and asked us to keep in touch. She had been to England for her midwifery training, as had several others; and they were delighted to share their memories with us.

We learned that several members of the church went to visit the sick and the elderly during the afternoon and then returned for the evening "Gospel Service". Such was their dedication and commitment to serve God. They were a real inspiration to us.

Reluctantly we left our new friends, who had even invited us to stay for Christmas and New Year! Knowing in our hearts we would return, we set off to cycle to "Santosa Island", just off the coast near Singapore harbour. Here we spent a relaxing afternoon on the beach and swimming in the sea. This place, we discovered, is the most southerly point of the continent of Asia!

The same evening, we set off for "Orchard Road", in the city centre, to see the Christmas lights. We used the very clean, efficient underground train system. We hadn't a clue what to do; so a young Chinese married couple came to our rescue and showed us how to use the ticket machine. It is similar to the London Underground, but different. We can't even remember now what we did!

The lights were the most amazing spectacle we have ever seen. They put even Blackpool in the shade! But more thrilling still was the powerful Christian witness there: All the Christian Churches had got together to praise, sing and dance in celebrating Christmas. There were Nativity scenes depicting all the ethnic groups of South East Asia and the Christians were distributing information regarding the Christmas services being held throughout Singapore City. The majority of these people were Chinese; but there were several hundred Malay and Indian people present, who were Muslims, Sikhs and Hindus.

Despite the huge crowd we were in (we could hardly move) we bumped into the couple we'd met at the station and then, having said goodbye for the second time, we met them again on the train "home"! They described themselves as "free thinkers" and said that their 10-year-old daughter attended the Christian Church with her friends because she enjoyed it! We encouraged them to go along; and we all hugged each other when we finally said "goodbye".

The following morning, we left our hotel and cycled to the North Coast Park, where we spent the day on the beach and swimming in the sea. From here we could see the coast of Malaysia; and we promised ourselves we would return again one day, in order to explore this interesting part of South East Asia.

After a relaxing day of "gentle" exercise we set off to cycle to Singapore airport, a journey of seven miles along the north coast of Singapore Island. Having checked in, with our luggage and bicycles safely taken care of, we were free to enjoy the luxury of the airport – the best we have ever experienced: there were tropical fish ponds surrounded by exotic shrubs, trees and plants, a live band playing Christmas carols, spectacular decorations and numerous shops to explore. There was even a large swimming pool, if you had the time to spare. In fact, it was almost a holiday in itself just being in this splendid place.

Thus, we left Singapore with many happy memories; and we are looking forward to going back, renewing our friendship with the Christians we have met there and taking the opportunity to cycle round Malaysia. We trust God we will return there soon.

Once we arrived in Wigan, on 21st December, it was truly good to be back and we really did rejoice in being embraced by our church family at St. Mark's on Christmas Day. We thanked God, from the bottom of our hearts, for our safe return.

Chapter Two

Malaysia: 2006

We set off from Manchester Airport with our bicycles, on Wednesday, 18th January 2006. We had cycled from our home in Worsely Mesnes to Wigan North Western station at 6 am on a cold, damp morning, wearing only our summer cycling clothes, which would be quite suitable for the tropical climate we were about to experience. Fortunately, our journey to the station was just over a mile and took us five minutes to complete; so we didn't get too cold! We caught the first train out of Wigan and arrived at the airport station an hour later, enabling us to check in at 7:30am for the 9am flight to Singapore.

Our journey took fourteen hours, crossing from one hemisphere into another and forward in time – an amazing experience, although very tiring! However, it was a pleasant flight, as we were served very graciously by the Malaysian air hostesses with drinks of every kind and delicious Indian vegetarian meals, which we had ordered when booking.

We arrived in Singapore on Thursday, 19th January and, with it being our second visit this time, we knew our way to the Chinese hotel where we had stayed before. Here we were greeted warmly by the owners who were delighted to see us again. Soon after our arrival we received a phone call from Elizabeth, an elderly Chinese lady whom we had met at church in December 2004 on our way back from New Zealand. We had already written to Elizabeth informing her of our visit; so she had been expecting us.

Half an hour later Elizabeth arrived and took us out for a delicious traditional Singaporean meal known as "fish head curry". She also took us out on a tour round the Geylang Road District showing us the various shops where you can buy good quality cheap clothing and also, more important to us, a nearby supermarket where we could purchase our food at a low cost. Elizabeth even took us to the underground station and bought us travel cards for the buses and trains in Singapore City – a very kind gesture indeed. Such was the kindness we received from our Christian brothers and sisters on the other side of the world.

Two days later, a married couple, also from the church, Catherine and Ming Seong, took us out, together with Elizabeth, for an Indian meal in a district known as "Little India". Not only did we receive food for our bodies, to prepare us for a 1,500-mile cycle tour of Malaysia, but also for our souls.

On the Friday evening, we had attended an excellent Bible study with our Chinese friends; and on Sunday we were at church from 9am to 2pm! This included "Sunday School" (a Bible study and discussion for adults as well as children), followed by breakfast, then a worship service, "Breaking of Bread" (i.e. Holy Communion) and a communal meal at 1pm. The latter was almost a banquet, as we celebrated the marriage of a lovely Indian couple, who had recently returned from their wedding in India.

Our brothers and sisters in Christ gave us a warm welcome and the assurance of their prayers as we set off to cycle the next day.

We left Singapore on Monday 23rd January and began our epic journey round the peninsula of West Malaysia. Singapore is an island, which contains the city itself; so in order to cross the border to Malaysia you have to cross a narrow strip of sea, by road bridge, to Johor Bahru, which is the first town you come to, situated in the state of Johor Bahru. There are two bridges; but one is a motorway; so we took the one we could cycle over. It was a wonderful experience to arrive in another country in South East Asia, having seen its coastline from Singapore's North Coast Park, just over a year ago, when we returned from New Zealand in December 2004.

On the first day of our tour we arrived in Skudai, about thirty miles north west of Johor Bahru; and discovered a cheap hotel where we could spend the night before setting off, early the next day, towards the west coast.

Most of the cheaper hotels in Malaysia are owned either by Chinese or Malay people. The Chinese-owned hotels are usually the more expensive, as they are very often equipped with a television as well as air-conditioning, whereas the Malay-owned hotels would only have electric fans and in very few rooms, a television. We were quite happy not to have air-conditioning, as it does not help you to adapt to the humid, tropical climate; and we did not need a television either. Thus, we could keep the cost down; and there were more Malay hotels than Chinese wherever we went, which suited our purpose.

It was very cheap to eat out and each evening, after booking into a hotel, settling in and having a shower at the end of a long day's cycle ride, we would enjoy the luxury of a cooked meal. A lot of meals were prepared in small cafes, with tables outside for eating; and the food would be traditional Malay cuisine, consisting of rice or noodles with a variety of vegetables and meat or fish. We enjoyed the Malay food very much and found it spicier than the

Chinese food, which from time to time we would also sample.

We provided our own breakfast each morning, consisting of bread, with either honey, peanut butter or jam, a supply of which we carried with us, replenishing our stocks when necessary. We also carried tea, coffee and drinking chocolate and used tinned condensed milk which we could buy quite easily from local shops.

Our midday meal also consisted of bread and, either one of the spreads, already mentioned, or bananas, which we could buy quite easily on most days from the numerous fruit stalls on the roadside. We ate plenty of fresh fruit of the tropical variety: mangoes, dragon fruit, papaya and pineapple – not only delicious, but also very nourishing.

We set off from Skudai and cycled to Melaka, on the west coast, in the state of Negeri Sembilan. On our way we met a very fit 78-year-old man from Denmark. He too was touring Malaysia on his bicycle. During the next five weeks we met very few European cyclists – only four in total; so it was good to spend some time with this man and share our experiences. He also gave us the address of a good, cheap hotel in Melaka where we could spend the night; and he was a great source of inspiration.

Melaka is a very interesting town, where the first Muslim settlers came to Malaya and brought their religion and culture to the indigenous people. It is still a thriving port today.

We soon settled into the hotel and were able to store our cycles safely on the balcony, by our room. The hotel rooms we stayed in throughout our journey were always clean, with fresh bed linen and towels provided, as well as an electric kettle and a shower. We had all we required and thanked God daily for His provision.

Every morning we would pray and ask for God's protection and guidance for the day ahead. We trusted Him to provide the food we needed for the day, as well as suitable accommodation at our journey's end; and He never let us down!

From Melaka we journeyed on to Port Dickson, which is a favourite seaside resort for the local people. Here we were able to have a rest day and enjoy relaxing in the sun and swimming in the sea. We were made very welcome at the Chinese-owned hotel, which was right by the sea, offering us excellent accommodation for only £3 a night! The landlady, Grace, showed a keen interest in the Christian faith and told us she enjoyed going to a local Bible study and prayer group. We were able to encourage her and promised to pray for her.

Feeling very refreshed, we continued our journey towards Kuala Lumpur, Malaysia's capital city. It was Sunday, 29th January,2006 and Chinese New Year's Day when we arrived; and we found ourselves worshipping God in the oldest Chinese Methodist Church in the country, right in the heart of the city. Here we were given a very warm reception by a clapping congregation of several hundred Chinese Christians. It was a very moving experience and far more exciting than our visit to the famous twin towers of almost 1400 feet in height!

We departed Kuala Lumpur with very happy memories, relieved to be back on our bikes, cycling through the rural areas and experiencing the traditional Malaysian way of life.

We continued to cycle along the west coast, where the Indian Ocean meets the shore, passing through Sengai Besar and then arriving at Pangkor Island the following day. Here we were greeted by a host of monkeys. They were everywhere, at the roadside, in the trees and sometimes blocking our path. It was an interesting experience!

We cycled on to Parit Buntar, where we hoped we would find some accommodation. (Our average daily distance was about 60 miles; but it could be more if we couldn't get somewhere to spend the night.) As we looked around we were approached by an Indian gentleman who had done some cycle touring (very rare among Malaysians!) and was happy to provide free accommodation, including excellent home-cooked Indian food, to any cycling tourist he met! We could hardly believe this to be true. But it was! David guided us to his house where we met his wife, a Dutch couple and an Irish girl, who were also touring Malaysia on bicycles.

We had an excellent time of fellowship together; and the next day went on our separate journeys. The Dutch couple had cycled from China, through Vietnam, Cambodia and Thailand; and were now on their way to Kuala Lumpur to fly to their home in Holland. The Irish girl stayed to enjoy a "rest day" and we cycled to Penang Island; further up the coast.

Arriving in George Town, the capital of the Island, we found the youth hostel, where we stayed two nights, so we were able to enjoy a well-earned day off from cycling, which we spent on a lovely white, sandy beach, relaxing and swimming in the sea. Chinese New Year was also being celebrated and, in the evening, we wandered through the streets of George Town, sampling freshly-cooked Chinese food from the numerous stalls. We had quite a feast! We also "bumped" into our Irish friend when we were there. It was good to know she was safe and sound!

We crossed back to the mainland by ferry and continued our cycle tour to the Thai border. We would love to have crossed over to Thailand; but we had been warned by the Dutch cyclists that there was a lot of fighting between the Muslims and Buddhists; therefore, it wouldn't be safe to go there at present. So we cycled across

Malaysia, through the mountains, to the east coast instead. This was quite an adventure!

Everywhere we went throughout our cycling tour of Malaysia we were greeted with "Hello! How are you?" It was mainly the young children, too young to have started school, who would run out of their wooden shacks, waving and calling to us. This was something we really missed when we first returned to England. We found it so quiet after Malaysia! However, this situation changed a few years later as we continued cycling round the world for different charities and became more well-known in our community. The schoolchildren living on our estate then continued where the Malaysian children left off!

The drivers of both motor cycles and cars would also wave to us and cheer us on our way. This was something we rarely experience in England, where most drivers want to get somewhere as quickly as they can and pretend we're not even there and an inconvenience for being in their way!

When we cycled across the top of Malaysia, through the mountains, we were very encouraged by the motorists and lorry drivers, especially when a lot of the route was a long arduous cycle, uphill for many miles through the monsoon rains. When it rains in Malaysia it rains indeed!

The further inland we went, the hillier it became. At one point, when asking some policemen the directions to the next village, because it was uphill for several miles, they said we couldn't do it! But, thank God, we did!

Further on our journey we experienced a very heavy downpour of rain, so much so we could hardly see our way ahead. However, we finally came down off the mountains to a village, where we could spend the night. This was in a traditional Malay-style wooden building, on stilts above a large swamp! Here was an ideal place for the Dengue Fever mosquito to thrive! This disease is not as serious as

Malaria; but it is more severe than the worst dose of Influenza. Fortunately, we didn't get it!

We continued cycling towards the East Coast, staying one night in Kota Bharu, a town near the Thai border. We then cycled along the beautiful shores of the South China Sea. This coast is less populated than the West Coast and much more traditionally Malay, with its rural way of life and bamboo homesteads, built on stilts to protect from flooding during the monsoon season.

All along the wayside the local people would be selling fruit and vegetables and even cooking delectable dishes for passers-by. Many of these people survive on a "rural economy", which means they can sell whatever they grow which is surplus to their requirements. As Malaysia is in the tropics and has plenty of rain as well as hot sunshine, it is a country with a very rich produce of a large variety of fruit and vegetables. There an also large plantations of olive palms, the oil of which provides a good source of income for the country.

Whenever we met the schoolchildren, as we cycled through the towns and villages, they delighted in practising their English, which they learned as a second language in primary school, as well as high school. "Hello how are you?"; "What is your name?" and "Where are you going?" is what they normally said. We soon got used to them asking the same questions! Often they would wave to us from the classroom windows, when we cycled passed the school buildings; we would wave back and hope they wouldn't be in trouble with their teachers!

Along the east coast we stayed at a place called Rantau Abang – a Nature Reserve managed by the Malaysian Government. It was a wonderful location and we had a well-earned rest day there, stopping at the home of Ramilee the Manager, his wife, 10-year-old daughter and elderly mother. There was accommodation provided for schoolchildren too, as it was used for educational visits.

The Nature Reserve consisted of a wetland area with a large river, which ran into the ocean and a vast rainforest. We thoroughly enjoyed exploring on foot, by canoe and even on a raft, using a rope to pull us across the river to the beach. There we were able to relax and swim in the sea, which could be very rough at times.

We had a marvellous send-off when we were ready to cycle to our next destination, with thirty-five Malaysian primary schoolchildren waving us "goodbye", looking very smart in their traditional Muslim dress.

Further along the east coast, at a place called Kuala Romping, whilst enjoying another rest day, walking along the shore through the palm trees, we encountered a large family enjoying their Sunday barbeque on the beach. They took no time in inviting us to join them and soon we were "tucking" into some delicious, traditional Malay food. The head of the family, a young man named Zeffrul, owned a large palm plantation at Selangdan and offered to take us there on a visit and, also, to the nearby Endau Romping State Park. We found both these places very interesting indeed.

There had even been an elephant stampede at the palm plantation the night before, destroying a large part of the forest; but fortunately no lives lost and nobody harmed in any way.

The State Park was very beautiful, with exotic, tropical plants abounding and stunning scenes of mountains and lakes.

There are three main ethnic groups in Malaysia, the majority being Malay, who are mostly Muslims. The others are either Chinese or Indian. These people are either Buddhists, Hindus or Sikhs. Very few are Christians; and these are mainly Chinese and a few Indians. The Muslim Malays are some of the kindest people we have met and all the Malaysians we met were very friendly and would often greet us with "Welcome to Malaysia!"

Malaysia is certainly a place well worth a visit and we shall never forget the wonderful experiences we had of the people, the country and most of all, God's grace and goodness to us.

Chapter Three

Malaysia and Thailand: 2007

In January 2007, we set off early in the morning, on a cold winter's day, to cycle to Wigan North Western station in order to catch the first train to Manchester Airport. Dressed only in summer cycling clothes we felt the cold; but we soon warmed up once on the train; and in one hour's time we were at the airport ready to check in before our flight to Singapore at 9am.

We do not put our cycles into boxes as we need them to cycle from our home in Worsely Mesnes to the station, which is just over a mile away. Then we need them again, on arrival at our destination, to be able to cycle into the city centre and find suitable accommodation for a night or two, which gives us time to prepare our trip and recover from jet lag. Once at the airport, all we need to do is to deflate the tyres a little; and then the bikes are ready to go into the hold of the plane. We also put some bubble-wrap around the pedals, secured with plastic bags, to prevent them from damaging any luggage, once they are stored. Most airlines will take our bikes, free of charge, as part of our luggage allowance; and we take full responsibility for how they are carried. They have never been seriously damaged – only sometimes a little scratched – on the numerous flights we have been on. The fact they can be seen, as opposed to being boxed, may help to ensure they are handled carefully.

We also travel very light, carrying only the minimum of luggage, which consists of two pannier bags each, carried on our rear carriers and usually, all together, weighing less than one person's allowance! With experience we have learned what we need to take with us and we have made a list, which we refer to each time we travel. We did take camping gear the first time we travelled overseas, which was to New Zealand; but, obviously, this means we have to carry more. Since then we have found the hotels in South East Asia very cheap and suitably equipped for our basic needs. They have cost the equivalent £3 a night on average. Also the food, including eating out, is very cheap and quite nutritious, as well as substantial for us cyclists.

Having checked in our bikes and luggage we were able to relax and spend some time exploring the airport, looking in the shops (without buying anything!) and enjoying a morning coffee before our flight. We had got up at 4am, so it seemed like mid-morning!

The flight from Manchester to Singapore was very pleasant and the Malaysian and Singaporean staff were as we had previously experienced: very kind, courteous and dressed elegantly, which goes a long way to inspire confidence in us passengers. The food was excellent: We chose Indian vegetarian for all our journeys and there were always plenty of drinks and snacks available during the fourteen-hour flight.

When we arrived, having travelled forward in time, we did feel quite weary; but the thirteen-mile cycle ride along the pleasant East Coast Park, towards the city centre of Singapore soon revived us and lifted our spirits. We had left mid-winter behind in England and here we were cycling along the coast of the South China Sea among beautiful palm trees bathed in tropical sunlight. It was quite heavenly!

Some of the journey was on busy main roads, the first one just a short way from the airport to the coastal park and then, when we left the coast, it wasn't very far to cycle to the Meng Yew Hotel, where we had stayed the previous year. The Chinese family, who owned the hotel, were delighted to see us again. This was now the fifth time we were staying there and we felt very much at home.

Once we had settled in, to what was to be our "home" for the next two days, we were met by Nancy and Tony, whom we'd first met at the Chinese Church, on our return from New Zealand just over two years ago. Nancy and Tony are a Chinese married couple who came to see us off at the airport when we flew back to England in December 2004. We saw them again when we travelled to Malaysia, via Singapore, in 2006. On our return from cycling around Malaysia they very kindly took us to Changi Village for a delicious Indian meal the night before we flew back to Manchester. So, by now, we had become firm friends.

We were still very tired but they insisted on taking us on a tour, using various buses, all over Singapore, as well inviting us to eat out in at least three different places! The food in Singapore is both varied and extremely delicious, with many dishes to choose from. The food is freshly cooked and traditional Indian, Malay or Chinese meals are in abundance. Their cooking certainly takes some beating! It is also very cheap; hence eating out in Singapore is a popular pastime, for many of its inhabitants as well as visitors.

The following day was Sunday which enabled us to be reunited with our Chinese brothers and sisters at the Changi Road Assembly, where we all worshipped the Lord. It was wonderful to see them again; and we were extremely touched by their loving hospitality. Once again we were lavished with their delicious Chinese food, at breakfast, after "Sunday School", at 10am and, again, after the main service, at 1pm.

During the service, when there was a time of prayer in both Chinese and English, many people prayed for us, especially that we would be kept safe on our journey through Malaysia to Thailand for the next few weeks.

We also saw Catherine and Ming, whom we'd first in 2004. Ming asked us to stay with them, on our return to Singapore, six weeks later. We were delighted to accept their invitation; and they gave us clear instructions on how to reach their home from the Malaysian Border.

Our original plan, on arrival in Singapore, had been to cycle in Indonesia. This would have meant us taking a ferry from Singapore to Sumatra. However, when we discussed this with one of the elders of the church, Michael, a former cyclist, we were advised against this as, apparently the roads were unsuitable and the place "teemed" with bandits. We might not have worried too much about the latter threat; but we did need to know that the roads would be reliable for a decent bicycle tour. Thailand was thus recommended as being a good place to cycle. As we hadn't planned to go there we didn't book a flight beyond Singapore; so, after some consideration, we decided to cycle through Malaysia and continue on into Thailand as far as time would allow, bearing in mind we were returning to Manchester six weeks later.

Although a sudden adaptation had to be made, we were quite pleased with the idea of returning to Malaysia; and the prospect of going on into Thailand was exciting. Thus we set off, happy to cycle through familiar territory, this time heading for the east coast, so we could return along the west coast – the reverse of what we did in 2006. We found the route along the west coast of Singapore Island also interesting, as before we had travelled along the east coast. We even saw the Far East BBC Broadcasting Station!

We crossed the border into Malaysia, via Johar Bahru, with no problem and then continued to Mersing, on the east coast of West Malaysia. This was quite a long journey – over one hundred miles; and we had to cycle a fair way in darkness. In the tropics it is usually dark by 7pm, which takes some time to get used to, as in England, when we have warm, sunny weather, the days are long and it is light for a long time in the evening.

We were able to find suitable low-cost accommodation in Mersing; and the following day we continued to Kuala Romping and found the Malay hotel where we had stayed the year before. The staff were delighted to see us again and we felt very much at home. It was also easy for us to find somewhere to eat that evening, being so familiar with the place.

As we cycled through the rural districts, with their traditional wooden and bamboo houses on stilts, we were greeted with numerous cries of "Hello!" from the young children, running out of their homes to the roadside. We often heard them before we even saw them! This made us feel very welcome in a country so far from home.

We were to have many more pleasant experiences of meeting people in Malaysia, some of whom we had met in 2006 and others for the first time. We certainly had no regrets in coming back to this warm, friendly country. One place will always remain in our memory. It was a lovely seaside resort called "Teluk Chempedak Beach", very popular among the Malaysian citizens. We spent the night at the Chinese-owned hotel, where we had stayed the previous year; and, when the owner – a very traditional, elderly Chinaman - saw us, the delight in his face was a joy to behold! He could hardly believe we were back again.

As we approached the border with Thailand, not far from the large town of Kota Bharu, an Australian man jumped out of his car and warned us not to go into Thailand! He told us that there was still a lot of fighting between the Muslims and Buddhists and we could be in danger! We respected his concern; but we told him our Chinese friends in Singapore were praying for us and that we trusted the Lord to protect us! He was somewhat surprised, but wished us "good luck!"

Once we had crossed over into Thailand by ferry and continued cycling on what was major trunk road running from Singapore right through to China, we were surprised to find how quiet it was after the busy road along the entire east coast of Malaysia. Not many miles further along we discovered why: There was a military blockade with several armed soldiers on guard duty. They were quite happy to see us and waved us on our way! We were now aware that there were evident problems in this part of Thailand.

Fortunately, we didn't come into contact with any hostility between the two rival forces; but there had been some serious incidents. We learned that there was a minority group of Muslims who wanted to control a province in the northern part of Malaysia, close to the border and three of the adjacent southern provinces of Thailand. The majority of the indigenous Thai people, being mostly Buddhist, were opposed to this.

However, we soon discovered as we travelled further on, that there were a significant number of Muslim Thai people who were quite happy to dwell in peace and harmony with their fellow countrymen who were Buddhists. We saw numerous examples of both groups of people living and working together wherever we went, as well as schoolchildren and young people mixing together freely in what were obviously close friendships. We found this very reassuring and hopeful for the future of Thailand.

We could always distinguish between the two groups by their clothes. The Muslim Thai people, as in Malaysia, wore traditional dress - both the men and women as well as the children - whereas the Buddhists dressed the same as most Westerners would in the tropical climate of Thailand – only a lot more colourfully!

As we were dressed, all the time we were cycling, in summer cycle wear, i.e. Lycra shorts and short-sleeved tops or, on our days off, in shorts and T-shirts, we never gave offence as both the Buddhist men as well as the women also wore shorts. In Malaysia the Chinese dressed in a similar fashion; thus our dress was always acceptable in both these countries.

We cycled through two of the southern provinces of Thailand, where there were hostilities and military blocks along the main coastal road; but we never experienced any conflicts during the week we spent travelling there.

While we were in Thailand the Jubilee of the King was being celebrated; and in all the towns' large pictures of him and his family were on display. The King was obviously well-thought of and we learned that he was the world's longest reigning monarch, our own Queen being the second!

Apparently, the King of Thailand encourages his subjects to make full use of the land; thus farming is a major industry and there is an abundance of fruit and vegetables grown there. These are sold in the markets and on numerous stalls along the major roads. We didn't have any difficulty in buying fresh fruit which we thoroughly enjoyed each day. On one occasion we were given a pineapple each when stopping at a place where they were grown. It was like nectar for a thirsty cyclist. Thirst-quenching and delicious they were; these pineapples were prepared so we could eat them immediately. They were a wonderful provision.

The Thais are also very resourceful and enterprising where cooking is concerned. In all the towns and along the wayside, trailers attached to bicycles were present with cooking facilities on board. These could be parked anywhere and the food was freshly cooked, spicy and delicious. In the towns, chairs and tables were placed on the footpaths, and here we would eat a hot meal each evening.

The Thai cuisine is similar to Malay, perhaps a little spicier and usually eaten with chopsticks, although spoons are always available for those less adept. We really enjoyed the food very much. On one occasion the waitress removed all the spices from our table saying we couldn't eat them! We soon removed her pre-conceptions by asking for them back!

Our first stop, once over the Malaysian border, was in Narathiwat where we found a cheap hotel built of wood with a balcony overlooking the river. We stayed in such places throughout our stay; but the memory of this is etched on our minds: It was our first stop in Thailand; and the sight of the fishermen in their traditional boats, early in the morning was so typical of their way of life. Also a Chinaman, staying on our floor, played "Amazing Grace" on his "penny whistle" soon after our arrival. He did this especially for us to make us welcome and we felt very blessed.

Later on, as we travelled into the next "troubled" province, we were stopped by a jeep in which there were about four police officers. They didn't speak a lot of English; but we understood they were very worried about us cycling through this part of the country; so they urged us to put our bikes on the back of their vehicle in order to transfer us safely to the border of the next province, about twenty miles away. We managed to convince them that we wanted to cycle and that we were doing it for charity. Eventually they let us go on our way but insisted on giving us an escort. We were deeply moved by their concern and very grateful for their protection. We were not even aware that they had followed us until we reached the border and they suddenly appeared and waved "goodbye"!

Throughout Thailand we experienced the friendly hospitality of the people. They were also very kind and courteous. The schoolchildren were delightful, always greeting us as they went to and from school, practising their English at the same time.

We passed many Buddhist Temples which were beautifully ornate and exquisitely designed. They were a picture to behold and a tribute to the devotion of the people, who so carefully preserved these buildings. We knew we were in Thailand and not Malaysia, where there are more mosques than temples.

Thailand is a land of many contrasts: we found it quite flat; so we were able to cycle, on average, ninety miles each day. However, there were mountains in the interior and we crossed these when we cycled from the east coast to the west as we commenced our return south to Singapore.

Along the west coast was where the Tsunami of 2004 occurred and, already, there had been extensive rebuilding of many of the hotels situated along the coast where most tourists from the West spend their holidays. As we cycled through such places we saw several Tsunami "Escape Routes". These were a sad reminder of what had happened just over two years ago.

We met one young man in a bus shelter, where we stayed in order to have something to eat, in the shade away from the sun. He worked at one of the hotels and he told us his story of how he had fled to the safety of the hills, inland, when he was aware of the impending disaster. He also told us how his family had been kept safe, as they lived in the interior away from the coast. We said how deeply sorry we were at the time and that, at our Church, we had prayed for them and sent money to help them rebuild their homes. The young man was very moved and said he thanked God for the help they had received and for keeping him and his family safe.

It did our hearts good to see how resilient these people were, following such tragic circumstances.

Very close to the border with Malaysia we stayed at a place called Satun. Here we found a Christian Church, the first we had encountered since our arrival in Thailand, where only 1% of the population are Christian. We were ready for a rest day; so we found suitable low-cost accommodation; and the following day, it being Sunday and, incidentally, Chinese New Year, we attended for worship. We were given a tremendous welcome by the Thai Christians. We were even invited to speak to them all and, as most of them spoke very little English, a Chinese lady, married to a Thai, whose English was excellent, translated for us.

The church building was full to capacity and decorated with beautiful coloured garlands throughout. There was a lot of hearty singing, praising and praying, a Bible reading, a sermon and Holy Communion. All this was conducted in the Thai language; but we felt quite at home, especially when we celebrated Holy Communion and gave each other the sign of peace in the traditional Thai fashion with hands together as in prayer. This was a very sacred moment - one which we will always treasure. Afterwards we were taken for a meal, in a local restaurant, to celebrate Chinese New Year. This was most enjoyable, with delicious Thai food and good Christian fellowship.

Our hardest day's cycling, during the whole trip, was across the mountains into Malaysia. The road seemed to climb forever! Once we did get to the top and back over the border, we really did need a break and something to eat. To our pleasant surprise we were greeted by a Malay family: a married couple with two children – a boy and a girl of school age. They had seen us cycling up the mountain road as they passed in their car and were very impressed by us! They invited us to join them for a meal "al fresco". This consisted of delicious roast chicken, rice, vegetables and fresh fruit. There was plenty for us all; so we "devoured" it with relish and thanked them for their kind generosity.

We cycled back along the west coast of Malaysia and, once again, we stopped at Port Dickson, where we had stayed the previous year. It was lovely to see Grace and her family and renew our friendship. Grace very kindly let us phone Catherine and Ming Sing in Singapore; so we could give them some idea of when to expect us. Two days later we reached Singapore and, as we went over the border from Johor Bahru onto the Island of Singapore, we experienced one of the heaviest monsoon rainfalls we had known. We arrived at Catherine and Ming's house soaked to the skin! However, Catherine soon had our clothes in her washing machine; fresh clothes and a welcoming meal of traditional Chinese food were provided. Catherine is an excellent cook!

We spent two days with our friends in their lovely home, situated in a very residential part of the city where the houses were once owned by the British officers, in the armed forces, when Singapore was a colony. In many ways the district had a distinct English "feel" about it; even the roads were named after our towns and villages. Overlying this was the obvious influence of the Asian culture, which was mostly Chinese. This is very much how it is in Singapore as a whole, which makes it such an interesting place to visit!

Our Chinese friends made us very welcome; we couldn't have felt more at home. It was lovely to see them and our friends at the church on Sunday. We were truly able to rejoice in the Lord, that we had returned safely – an answer to their prayers and ours!

Chapter Four

India: 2008

"A Land of Many Contrasts"

In February, 2008 we flew to Chennai (formerly known as "Madras") in South India. We set off from Manchester, stopping at Qatar, for a few hours "en route". This was our first time to fly with this airline; and we were very impressed with the treatment we received: The staff were kind and courteous, even providing large plastic bags in which to transport our cycles. The food on board was excellent, (we chose Indian vegetarian) a variety of drinks could be ordered and snacks were distributed throughout the long journey.

Qatar Airport is very modern, large and with good facilities. Free meals are provided to passengers spending more than an hour when changing flights, and there is free internet access. It is on a par with Singapore Airport, but not as ornate or aesthetically pleasing. However, it has only been built quite recently and is still being developed.

On the flight, from Qatar to Chennai, Jan struck up a conversation with an Indian lady, "Nythia", who was sitting beside her and was on her way home, after visiting her two daughters living in America. Nythia told us that her husband, "Ram", would be meeting her at Chennai Airport; and said that we would be welcome to stay with them until we were ready to set off on our journey. Nythia and Ram had also travelled extensively; but not on bicycles! Our trip consisted of a 1,500-mile cycle tour of the southern peninsula of India.

Once we had arrived at the airport, collected our bikes and luggage and inflated the tyres, we found ourselves surrounded by a large crowd of Indian men. They were fascinated by the sight of two English people preparing to cycle in India, on bicycles very different from what they were accustomed to seeing. In India it is mainly poor people who ride bikes; and these are similar to our old-fashioned "roadsters" – once upon a time a common sight in England, before so many owned motor cars. They were intrigued by the gears and computers; and couldn't resist touching them, despite our protests!

Finally, we were able to follow Ram and Nythia in their car, for a journey of approximately 10 miles, at 4am, when it was still quite dark. It was a shock to us just how noisy the traffic was and the amount of it, so early in the morning. For the next six weeks this would be our experience, which we never really got used to!

Our other experience of "culture shock" was having to endure "patiently" the endless questions the men and boys persisted in asking, everywhere we went. This wasn't easy when you have been asked the same thing all day, after cycling 60 miles in a very hot climate. These questions consisted of "Where are you going?", "Where do you come from?", "What is your name?" and "How many children do you have?" We often wished we had a recorded message we could switch on each time!

Of course, we did realise that it was their way of being friendly; but, by English standards, it was being "nosey"! The women and girls were far less inquisitive and, therefore, it seemed to us, more polite. This, however, was because their status and role in society was different; but not, necessarily inferior to that of the men and boys.

Every time we stopped for a short break we would be surrounded by a large male audience, sometimes talking and often just staring at us! We very rarely had a "quiet" break anywhere!

When we arrived at the home of Nythia and Ram we were amazed at the size of their house. Never before, or since, have had we stayed in such a grand place. It was truly like a small palace. The rooms were large and spacious, furnished lavishly and very ornate. The house had three storeys, was surrounded by beautiful gardens and, on the roof, there was a large terrace on which there were many plant pots filled with exotic tropical plants and flowers.

Nythia and Ram are "Brahmins", the name given to the top caste of Hindus; and as such, they are strict vegetarians and very devout. They even had a room reserved to "house" all their "gods". These were various Hindu deities, which they worshipped as part of their religious practise. They were very happy to entertain us and we were given marvellous hospitality, which included some delicious Indian vegetarian meals. We were very grateful, indeed; and thanked God for these lovely people.

We spent two nights at the home of Nythia and Ram; so we had a day in which to explore Chennai. Nythia very kindly drove us around the city; so we could see some of the main attractions. We visited two very beautiful temples, and a huge open market, stretching from the main road and across the wide beach, almost to the sea. Here we saw the Indian Ocean for the first time, situated on the east coast, in the Bay of Bengal.

Along this same beach, at the edge of the city, can be found small "shanty towns", consisting of makeshift homes, made from cardboard, corrugated iron and plastic sheets, or anything else suitable. Adequate sanitation and running water was non-existent; such was the extreme poverty of Nythia and Ram's neighbours.

The following morning we set off on our journey, which, for the next six weeks, took us along the east coast, as far as Kanyakumari at the southernmost point of India; and then along the west coast, as far as Mangalore and back to Chennai, via Bangalore. We travelled through four states: Tamil Nadu, Kerala, Karnataka and Pradesh – a total distance of 1,500 miles.

Our trip to India really opened our eyes. Cycling in South India through four large states, each with a different language, enabled us to meet a great many people, living in so many varied ways, from the very rich to the very poor.

We met people living in very simple village huts, as they must have done for centuries, with oxen as their beasts of burden and a "hand to mouth" existence from their plots of land. These people were mainly Hindu and belonged to the lowest caste; they often lacked basic health care and most had very little education.

In sharp contrast were the well-educated, with Masters Degrees, working in varying professions and having a very high standard of living. Many of these were the high caste Hindus, and Christians. The Christians, often from Hindu backgrounds, had equal chances of education, unlike the low-caste Hindus. Therefore they can make progress, however poor their beginnings.

What gave us great joy (and heartbreak) was to meet the many orphaned children. These children came from low-caste Hindu backgrounds and were being educated in boarding schools, run by the Christian Church. Some had been orphaned as a result of the Tsunami of 2004, others by the death of their mothers at, or soon after childbirth, due to the poor conditions in which they lived and a lack of adequate maternity care.

At one Pentecostal Church, the pastor and his wife had given a home to twenty-five young girls, victims of the Tsunami, who would have been left to die, or "sold "into the sex-trade, had they not been rescued (girls are not considered as "valuable" as boys in the rural area where they came from). These girls are now being educated in English-medium schools and have become Christians; so they now have the chance to earn their living and do something useful with their lives.

The future of India is truly in their hands; and we will pray for these young people, that they will continue to follow the Lord Jesus, in whom they have put their trust; and discover His purpose for their lives.

".... God will meet all your needs...." (Philippians 4: 19)

Our time in India was not so much a holiday as a pilgrimage of faith. Indeed, the main purpose of our journey was to make contact with the Christian Church and to be able to meet our brothers and sisters in Christ, have fellowship with them and discover what they were doing to serve the Lord in their part of the world.

This was a very rewarding experience: Whereas there is only 10% attendance at Sunday church worship in our so-called Christian country, approximately 99% of the Christian Indians, in a country where the majority are Hindu, will attend Church on a regular basis (the remaining 1% are either too frail or very ill). What is more, their services last from one and a half to three hours! All ages are represented and the choirs consist of, at least, twenty (usually more) people, most of whom are under twenty–five years of age. We were very inspired by their dedication and devotion.

The letter of introduction, which our vicar had given us before we left, explaining the main reason for our visit, was worth its weight in gold. On one occasion, after cycling sixty-five miles in horrendous traffic conditions, we were admitted to the private residence of the Bishop of the Diocese of South Kerala, after we had brandished our letter to the various officials "on guard", stating we had a letter from the Diocese of Liverpool, England! The Bishop took no time in arranging accommodation for that night in a private apartment, adjoining the local Church Boarding School for girls. There we were looked after very well by the staff, given two hearty meals and had the opportunity to meet the pupils, all of which we enjoyed very much.

This was our experience throughout our trip. We were given another letter of introduction, from the Pastor, Alex, at one of the Churches where we stayed, which also helped for the provision of accommodation. This was in Kochin where Alex's cousin lived. Unfortunately, she had visitors; so she arranged for us to stay in a luxury hotel, which for us was like a palace! We felt like Paul and Barnabus, in the Bible, on one of their missionary journeys; and praised God for His steadfast love.

"Always keep on praying for all the Saints" (Ephesians 6:18)

During the time we were in India we certainly experienced the power of prayer: we knew all our friends at home, especially at St. James' Church and the Indian Christians we met on our journey of faith, were praying for us.

Cycling in India was a horrendous experience: Not only was it extremely noisy, with the vehicles sounding their horns continuously; but the driving was very dangerous indeed. In fact, we would have felt safer cycling on the M6 than along a rural road in India, which was even noisier!

On one occasion, on a roundabout in a busy city, John was knocked off his bike by a taxi, signalling one way and driving the other! He was badly shaken, slightly concussed and his helmet was split in two! Jan, after making sure John had recovered sufficiently to be left alone, very quickly discovered a shop which sold car accessories. She told the staff what had happened; and two ladies took an unopened tube of glue off one of the shelves and proceeded to repair John's helmet. They made a very good job of it too- free of charge- enabling us to complete the next 1000 miles!

We thanked God for giving John the strength of heart, mind and body to continue cycling for several miles to our next place of rest. However, three days later he was admitted to hospital with severe dehydration, caused by drinking impure water. Once again, our faith was put to the test. Jan sent an email to our Vicar, Hilary; and the congregation of St. James' Church, together with that of the local Church, with whom we had made contact, prayed earnestly for John.

Simon, the Priest at the Church in Tuticorin, (in Tamil Nadu on the East coast) was an angel sent by the Lord: He came with us to the hospital and assisted with translation, as well as sending members of his congregation with food and drinking water each day. The hospitals in India generally do not supply food to the patients as they do in England. We should be very grateful for our National Health Service!

Life certainly wasn't easy for us a lot of the time; but our faith in God and in the power of prayer was immensely strengthened, we also experienced wonderful hospitality with the pastors and their families, at all the churches we visited.

As St. Paul exhorted the Christians at Ephesus to pray; so we wanted to urge our Christian friends in England to pray for their brothers and sisters in India, as they continue to pray for us.

"For we are God's Fellow Workers" (1 Corinthians 3:6)

Our trip to India was, indeed, a pilgrimage and, definitely, a journey of faith. We needed only a change of clothes (not many required in such a hot climate) our Bible, basic food items and bicycle tools and, of course, a map of South India. Our map was somewhat outdated; but we managed to travel 1.500 miles without getting lost!

There was also sufficient money in our bank account to cover the cost which, apart from the air fare, wasn't a considerable amount. Approximately £3.50 per day would provide all our food, including one cooked meal and overnight accommodation, in a cheap hotel with basic facilities. We trusted God to guide us and He never let us down!

It wouldn't be true to say that cycling in India was an enjoyable experience, as it was far too dangerous and stressful to be described thus. However, it did bring us into contact with the people, in a way that no other form of transport could. Our richest and most pleasurable times were those spent with our Indian brothers and sisters in the Lord.

With two exceptions, we were given hospitality and attended worship, whenever possible, at the Church of South India (C.S.I.), which is part of the worldwide Anglican Communion. The exceptions were the Indian Pentecostal Church, where we attended a service on our first Sunday, and St. Mary's Roman Catholic Cathedral in Bangalore, where we were given accommodation, food and a very warm welcome by Father Anthony, the Priest-in-charge. He even gave us a sum of money, which was sufficient for our food and overnight stay in Indian hotels, for the next two days, by which time we were back in Chennai.

It was at the Pentecostal Church we met Pastor Paul and his wife Jayaseeli, who are running an orphanage for twenty-five young girls, who had been victims of the Tsunami in 2004. They made us very welcome and invited us back to their home for a delicious meal; and we spent the rest of the day with them, visiting the orphanage, meeting the girls and enjoying being with their family, which included their two lovely young daughters, Paulin and Parvin.

Simon, the Priest at the C.S.I. Church in Tuticorin (where John was admitted to hospital) gave us the address of the C.S.I. School for the Deaf, where we stayed at the next stage of our journey. It was very interesting to meet the principal, her staff and many of the pupils. Here, not only were they being given a good education by special needs teachers; but they were introduced to the Christian faith. Most of the children came from very poor Hindu villages, where the teachers would go and convince the parents that their deafness would not disappear; and that they could teach and prepare them for their future lives as adults. It cost only £80 per year to give such a child their board and keep.

We learned, from the other Pastors we met, how much of their work was among the poor village people, not only in evangelising, but in practical ways, such as providing food for those unable to work and enabling the children to attend school. For just £50 a year it is possible to provide board and lodging, school uniform and books for such a child. Education itself is provided free by the Indian Government.

Another memorable experience was when we cycled along the east coast of Tamil Nadu, where the Tsunami happened; and we came across "The East Coast Community Project". We were invited to meet the primary schoolchildren, who were all orphaned as a result of the Tsunami in 2004. They were being given a good education in a wooden shack, using chalk and boards to do their lessons and sitting at old wooden benches, similar to those we had at primary school! When we met them they all stood up and saluted us! It was such a joy and great privilege to meet these children and all the dedicated staff.

The headmaster and teachers are well-qualified, but lack many of the modern facilities we have in England. They receive some money from the Indian Government; but they also rely heavily on charitable donations.

Two years prior to our trip to India we had met Grace and John, at St. Mark's Church in Newtown, Wigan, where we regularly worshipped for several years, before moving to St. James', in our own Parish. Grace and her husband John are retired primary school teachers; and had come to England for a year to visit their two sons and their families in Wigan.

When we told them we planned to cycle in South India they insisted that we stayed with them during our visit. So we kept in touch, both with Grace and John and their sons and daughter-in-laws until we were ready to set off on our journey.

Grace and John live in a very rural area of Kerala in a remote village. Yet we were able to find them! We stayed with them for five days; and we were able to celebrate Easter with the local Christian community at their Church, where Alex was the pastor.

This was a wonderful provision for us as, after already cycling 1000 miles and John's admission to hospital, we were ready for a rest!

The State of Kerala in South India is very unique insomuch that 50% of the population are Christian and 80%

66

are university graduates. There is, therefore, quite a high standard of living here and many of the houses are very well-built and quite magnificent to look at, with large, beautiful gardens surrounding them.

It should be said here, that the low-caste Indians, with very little or no formal education, who live in the rural areas appeared a lot better off than their contemporaries in the "shanty towns" of the towns and cities. These people live in traditional houses, made from mud and wattle, with thatched roofs made from straw. They also have land on which to grow food sufficient for their needs and keep livestock.

Their main problem was a lack of general health and, especially, maternity care. There was also very poor sanitation. For example, there would be only one latrine for a whole village and no running water. The local river, or lake, was used for washing clothes, bathing and to provide for cooking and drinking!

We saw several people who had "burnt-out" leprosy (i.e.no longer active), which had reaped havoc with their bodies; and many who were crippled as a result of broken limbs which had not been set properly. For these unfortunate people, medical care was unaffordable.

There was also a considerable lack of adequate refuse disposal and everywhere we went, especially in the towns and cities, there were huge amounts of rotting rubbish. We would occasionally see someone with a dust-cart and a hand-brush attempting to "clean-up", hardly effective for such a densely populated country!

We thought it would be a good idea for the government to provide the kind of refuse disposal we have in Britain; and this would also give paid employment to so many poor people. The Indian Government has enough money to do this; but it requires the political will to implement.

Whilst cycling in a very rural part of Kerala, a few miles away from the next town, where we intended spending the night, we were approached by two young men on a motor bike. They asked us all the usual questions, including, "Where are you going?" However, they were exceedingly helpful, not only in giving precise directions but, without us knowing, an escort – following us on their motorbike for about 20 miles!

When these two "Angels" eventually revealed themselves, they duly invited us to visit the home of one of them and have a rest and a cool drink. We politely declined their invitation, explaining that we wanted to reach our destination for that day, before it was dark. However, they insisted we needed a rest. This was, no doubt, very true; and we were also a lot older than them. We discovered great respect for the elderly in Asia; and we became aware that we now belonged to this group of people! In Thailand we were even called, affectionately, "Mama and Papa"!

On our arrival at the house we were greeted very warmly by James' mother, whose English was limited, as was her son's. Thomas, the other young man, spoke English fluently and he was able to translate when necessary. James' mother was a lovely Christian lady; she made us extremely welcome and offered to put us up for the night. It was beginning to get dark and we were quite tired by now; so we gladly accepted her offer.

We were provided with a very comfortable room for the night and, after a welcome hot shower and a substantial meal, which we thoroughly enjoyed. In the morning, after a good breakfast, we felt refreshed and replenished, ready to set off for the next stage of our journey.

Incidentally, Thomas confessed that he and his friend had deliberately invited us to stop for a while; so they could persuade us to stay the night! Such was the kind hospitality we were given during our time in India.

We promised all those dear and dedicated Christian people that we would alert our church to their needs when we returned home. Most importantly of all are our prayers, which they value tremendously, as they are working in extremely difficult conditions. Also we wanted to give financial support, knowing that the money would be put to good use and not wasted in unnecessary administrative costs. As I write, five years later, the school, on the east coast of Tamil Nadu, has almost been completely rebuilt; and soon the pupils will be educated in a building well-equipped to provide for all their educational needs. This is, indeed, an answer to all our prayers!

At the end of our journey, we were able to stay five days at Chennai Cathedral. It was Nythia and her husband, Ram, who arranged this for us. On our arrival in Chennai we contacted them at their home and were a given a very warm reception. They were overjoyed to see us as they had been very worried about our safety on the roads. Ram even confessed that he only drove his car in Chennai; and would make all other journeys by plane or train!

Unfortunately, Nythia wasn't in very good health and was waiting for an operation. However, they insisted on taking us out for a meal and then finding some suitable accommodation with Christians (their choice!) until we left India. So they contacted the cathedral and it was all arranged. We were, needless to say, very grateful to them.

The cathedral was truly a haven for us: we were able to stay there, without having to venture out into the noise of the traffic and the hustle and bustle of Indian city life, until it was time to cycle to the airport and travel home. The cathedral was set in large, spacious gardens as big as park; so it was quiet and peaceful, enabling us to rest mentally, as well as physically.

We were given lovely hospitality by Premraj and his wife Deborah, also an ordained priest. Together with their two children, Adythia, a boy of 14 and Amrutha, a girl aged

69

8, we were made to feel part of the family; and we enjoyed our stay with them very much.

While we were staying with Premraj and his family, a lady from "The Times of India" (a national newspaper equivalent to our "Times" in England) came to interview Deborah. This was because, in India, there are very few ordained women in the Christian Church; so Deborah, being one of the few, was of particular interest to this female reporter.

Once she had been interviewed, Deborah mentioned our cycle tour; so we had our turn, much to our surprise! We also had several photos taken of us with our bikes. This was on the day before we left India and returned to England; so we didn't think any more about it.

A few weeks later, when visiting Jan's mother in a nursing home in Woking, Surrey, we met one of the Sisters, who had recently returned from visiting her family in Kerala, South India. When she saw us she exclaimed that she had "seen an article and our photo in the paper". It wasn't until we returned to our home in Wigan that we realised that it had to have been in the "Times of India" and not a local Woking newspaper!

When it was time to leave Chennai and return home we were escorted to the airport by two young men on the staff of Premraj and Deborah. One cycled in front and one at the back, in order to protect us from erratic drivers! We were very grateful indeed, as our journey consisted of 10 miles of cycling in the dark along very busy roads. On arrival at the airport we thanked these two dear men and we embraced one another, as we said "goodbye".

We left India with many very happy memories of meeting such lovely people, even though we cannot recommend it for cycle touring! We truly thanked God for bringing us back home safe and sound!

Chapter Five

Thailand Revisited: 2010

"For we walk by faith and not by sight"
(2 Corinthians 5:7)

How true this verse from the Bible was for us during our six-week cycle tour of south Thailand in February and March, 2010. We had to depend on the Lord for everything: There we were with our cycles and just four pannier bags, in which we carried a few clothes, a basic food supply and spare inner tubes.

Each day we set off, very early in the morning, having prayed we would find food for our journey and a bed for the night. Our prayers were always answered: We received what we needed, not necessarily what we wanted. For example; a cold beer would have gone down very well in the heat of the day; but in temperatures of $90+^0$ F safe drinking water albeit lukewarm, by the time we drank it from our bicycle bottles, was absolutely vital to prevent dehydration, whereas beer wouldn't.

Our needs were met in most unexpected ways: On one occasion we hadn't seen bananas (which, together with bread, formed our staple diet) for over forty miles; and we hadn't eaten since breakfast at 6am! Then, just as we were beginning to flag, a banana stall miraculously appeared! Not only did we buy a huge bunch for a small price, the lady gave us an extra bunch free of charge! We now had sufficient bananas for the next three days!

We cycled onwards and prayed we'd find another fruit stall, with more choice; and "lo and behold" we discovered a stall laden with large watermelons for sale! This was just what we needed to refresh our thirst. We asked the man to cut one in half, which would have been more than enough; and he insisted on giving us the other half free! We certainly had an abundant supply that day.

Another miracle, among many, was when Jan became ill after eating chicken the night before. As we cycled further on her condition deteriorated and, just as she was in desperate need of a toilet, we passed through a village where there was a Christian mission. This was in a country where only 1% of the population are Christians! Jan's needs were ministered to by two lovely Thai women who laid her on a mattress, switched on a fan and gave her some refreshing drinks. This was, of course, after she had used their (very clean, hygienic) toilet.

When Jan had recovered a little these two ladies prayed for her in their mother tongue and then gave her a traditional Thai massage! This was very invigorating – both spiritually and physically. After resting for an hour we were able to continue our journey, covering over seventy miles! Jan certainly received the strength she needed for that day.

The work at the Mission, where we had received such care, was engaged in looking after young children, who had either been orphaned as a result of the 2004 Tsunami or were victims of domestic abuse. We assured the two young women of our prayers and thanked them from the bottom of our hearts.

Although we had visited Thailand before, in 2007, we discovered places we'd not seen before, as well as returning to parts we had already been to. It was still a very new experience for us, especially visiting Bangkok for the first time. We also ventured into Burma – more about that later.

When we returned to Bangkok, at the end of our journey, we had great difficulty trying to find the airport. We found ourselves going round in circles, during the rush hour – not be recommended in Bangkok, especially on a bicycle! We were trying to follow the various directions we had been given, feeling very frustrated and tired, having already cycled seventy miles that day.

Eventually, we stopped and prayed. Almost immediately an Englishman appeared! He was only the second person we had met from England during the whole time we were in Thailand; and he was able to give us precise directions to the airport! This was, indeed, an answer to our prayer!

The other English person we met (another "Angel" from the Lord?) was a fellow cyclist from Manchester, whom we met staying at the same place as us. He was able to inform us that we needed to extend our visas for another two weeks, in order for us to complete our journey. The permits we had stamped on our passports, on arrival in Thailand, lasted for only four weeks. We had just a day left! We had no time to lose, unless we were willing to be fined £10 each for every day they were overdue, which would have amounted to £280 in total.

We had been in complete ignorance of this fact, not having once looked at our passports. So, the next day we duly cycled to the border town of Ranong which, as it happened, was on our way! Here we took a boat to Burma to get our passports stamped for a further two weeks. This was on the last day of our four-week entry permit; but it was well-worth it, costing only £20, as opposed to paying a substantial fine.

Our day-trip to Burma was, in itself, an interesting experience: not only did we have a well-earned "rest day", but we also met a few fellow travellers from Britain; and it was good to be able to share our individual stories with one another. It was also a very pleasant journey on the boat; thus we relaxed and enjoyed it. The Thai people, who are mostly Buddhists, are extremely kind and hospitable. They made us feel very welcome; and their smiling faces and friendly greetings encouraged us immensely, as we cycled long distances, of up to eighty miles a day, in the tropical climate. We were also spurred on by the fact that we were doing this bike ride to raise money for "The Brick" – a charity for the homeless people in Wigan, where we live.

We returned to Singapore and spent a few days there, experiencing the kind hospitality of our Chinese friends, Catherine and Ming, at their home. It was also good to meet our brothers and sisters, in Christ, at the Changi Christian Assembly, who gave us, as always, a very warm welcome. Reluctantly, we left the warmth of their friendship and the climate of Singapore to return to Manchester. However, it was good to back home again, safe and sound.

"London Bridge" on the Great Ocean Road, Victoria, Australia.

Adelaide, South Australia.

Traditional rural accommodation on the east coast of West Malaysia.

Travelling towards the east coast of West Malaysia through the mountains of the north.

Outside an ornate Buddhist temple, in West Malaysia.

The paddy fields near Kota Bharu, West Malaysia.

Mission Bay on Lake Taupo, North Island, New Zealand.

Arriving at Wellington, North Island, on the ferry from Picton, South Island.

On the road at Franz Josef (glacier in background), South Island, New Zealand.

Lake Hawea, South Island, New Zealand.

Arriving from British Columbia, Canada to Washington, United States of America.

Golden Gate Bridge, San Francisco, California.

Singapore city centre: River Singapore at High Street.

John outside the famous Raffles Hotel in Singapore's city centre.

With our Asian brothers and sisters at the Changi Christian Assembly, Singapore.

BBC Far Eastern Relay Station, on the Kranji Reserve, Singapore.

En route to climb the "Lion's Head", Cape Town, South Africa. (Table Mountain in the background.)

John with the children at the African Church in Joubertina, Cape Province, South Africa.

The ocean and mountains of Cape Province, South Africa.

Exploring a Thai street market.

Enjoying a rest in Thailand.

Buddhist temple in Thailand.

Chapter Six

Australia: 2011

Cycling "Down Under"

In mid-February 2011 we set off with our bicycles and flew to Melbourne, Australia, via Singapore. This was our first visit "Down Under"; and it was an experience we will never forget. It was tough, but very enjoyable, nevertheless.

We had intended to cycle in Australia in 2009. However, John developed pneumonia during the 'flu epidemic that winter; and was unfit to travel. This proved, for us, a blessing in disguise, despite our profound disappointment, as it was in early 2009 that there was a spate of forest fires in the state of Victoria, where we had planned to cycle.

There was much devastation, with loss of life and the homes of many completely destroyed. Certainly, these unfortunate people were in our prayers at the time and we thanked God for His timely intervention, preventing us from going to Australia.

We were very pleased to be travelling via Singapore, where we planned to stay for a few days, enjoying a happy re-union with our friends there. The last time we'd visited was in 2010, when we travelled to Thailand; so this would be our ninth visit!

We also had the opportunity to see our Chinese friends in Melbourne, with whom we stayed for a few days, before and after our cycle tour of Australia: Pui Fun, a retired nurse who had trained in London, where Jan met her over thirty years ago. We had both met her and Chee Keong, her husband, last year when they visited Singapore and came to see us at the home of Catherine and Ming, where we were staying.

Staying with Pui Fun and Chee Keong also gave us a chance to explore the city of Melbourne and to be able to plan our forthcoming trip.

We were away for six weeks altogether; and spent four of these cycling, 1400 miles, in the states of Victoria and South Australia. Our journey took us along the coast of Victoria, including the famous "Great Ocean Road" and the coast of South Australia, as far as Adelaide.

Whilst in Adelaide, we were able to look up two of Jan's uncles, whom she hadn't seen for many years. Uncle Dennis and Uncle Brian are two of Jan's late mother's younger brothers, who emigrated to Australia several years ago, with their wives and children, some of whom were born in Australia. They are now great grandparents; so their families have significantly increased.

First, we called to see Uncle Brian and his wife, Pam. They weren't in at the time; so we left our bikes outside their house and went for a little walk. We returned a quarter of an hour later and, in the meantime, they had come back. They had no idea we were in Australia until they saw our bikes! Of course, they were delighted to see us; and we had a very happy re-union, with John meeting them for the first time.

After some time, we went in search of a "backpacker" hostel in a nearby seaside resort, which Uncle Brian recommended. Here we spent two very well-earned, "proper" rest days in a very comfortable, reasonably- priced hostel, conveniently situated near all the big shops and the beach. We were there for the weekend; so we were able to find a nearby church for Sunday worship. We were given a very warm welcome there and many of the congregation contributed generously to the charity for which we were doing our cycle tour.

We also had a wonderful time, relaxing on the sun-soaked beach and swimming in the sea. This enabled us to recover from all the cycling we had done so far; and it prepared us for our return journey to Melbourne. We were now halfway into our tour and very pleased with the progress we had made, for which we truly thanked God.

Before we set off to make our return journey, we cycled from the hostel, to Jan's Uncle Dennis where he lived with his wife Maureen in a suburb of Adelaide. To our great surprise Uncle Brian and his wife Pam were there too; so we had a truly grand reunion!

It hadn't been long since Jan's mother had died; so this meeting with her brothers was extra special, as it hadn't been possible for them to have attended the funeral. Reluctantly, we left them to continue our long journey, back to Victoria and Melbourne.

Before we did this, we made a slight detour to enable us to visit Adelaide – a really beautiful city and well worth making the extra effort for. We had a photo taken of us both together; and then we made our way to where we stayed for the night. It was a very historic German settlers' town called Hahndorf, about sixty miles away. There we were able to find a chalet, on a large campsite, just before it was dark and had a very comfortable overnight stay.

We returned to Melbourne on an inland route, through the wine-growing areas. The scenery was varied – flat, undulating and, sometimes quite hilly - very different from the spectacular "Great Ocean Road", where we had seen the "Twelve Apostles" and "London Bridge". These were unusual rock formations arising out of the sea and really quite magnificent. The coast of South Australia was different again; but still very scenic, with its vast bays and large expanses of ocean.

Once again, as we have experienced on previous cycle tours, we proved God's goodness and abundant provision. Each day, as we set off to cycle distances of sixty to ninety miles, we trusted the Lord to provide accommodation at the end of our journey. He never let us down!

On one occasion, after cycling over sixty miles in a very strong headwind, we arrived at our destination only to find there was "no room at the inn!" Everywhere in the small town of Beaufort, Victoria, was full. This was due to there being a large agricultural show taking place that weekend.

We would have had to cycle a further thirty miles to the next town and, quite honestly, we'd had enough! We prayed earnestly; and just as John was about to go and thank the manager of the holiday park, who had been ringing round all the possible places which offered accommodation, his wife had a sudden inspiration. She remembered just one more possibility; and on the spur of the moment she made a phone call:

It turned out to be a "Bed and Breakfast" with a difference! An elderly couple (about the same age as us), who were entirely self-sufficient vegans (and, incidentally Seventh Day Adventists) were endeavouring to introduce their customers to an alternative lifestyle of healthy living.

Dear Reader, you may think they didn't need to work so hard on us. To the contrary! Drinking tea and coffee (not to mention alcohol!) and eating dairy products was an anathema to them. We were also considered "heretics", because we worshipped God on a Sunday and not Saturday!

However, our stay with these dear people was quite an enjoyable experience: our first experience of their genuine kindness was when we had some difficulty in finding their house. We left the holiday park with clear directions on how to find the accommodation they had booked for us, which was about five miles away. However, we needed to turn off the main road after two miles; and then we continued along a very rough, unsurfaced road for three miles, before reaching our destination. Just as we were beginning to feel lost, the couple, with whom we were going to stay, appeared suddenly, from around a bend, to greet us and extend a warm welcome!

We had a comfortable bed for the night, preceded by a refreshing, hot shower. And, in the morning we were provided with a sumptuous vegan breakfast – ideal for cyclists, with plenty of energy food, including a large bowl of porridge. All this was free of charge; so we could contribute the money towards the charity for which we were doing this bike ride, namely, our local Community Youth Club, in Worsely Mesnes.

After breakfast, when we had said our "goodbyes," we were given various items of food to take with us; and, as they hugged us both, we felt they genuinely embraced us as their Christian Brother and Sister! They had even invited us to say "grace" at breakfast, for which we felt quite privileged.

Returning to Melbourne we experienced a warm, dry and sunny climate, most of the time. It was like a pleasant English summer. The months of February and March, when we were there, are the equivalent of our late summer. The State of Victoria has a temperate climate, whereas in South Australia it is a Mediterranean one. We found it a lot hotter there; but there was always a refreshing breeze, especially along the coast.

During the six weeks we were away, the four spent actually cycling included some "rest days". It wasn't strictly true to call these thus, because we used them to explore the places where we stayed, sometimes walking several miles. We also took the opportunity to swim outdoors, in the sea and mountain lakes. And we climbed two mountains from where we had spectacular views of the coastal plains of Victoria. However, as they say, "a change is as good as a rest!"

We found the Australians to be very kind, friendly and generous people. At most places, where we stayed, we were given discounts; and some accommodation completely free of charge. We even had a free dental check-up in Melbourne! This was done, very thoroughly, by Chee Keong, Pui Fun's husband.

On our last night, before arriving back in Melbourne, we were given three pints of beer and a luxury room for the night, "on the house"! All this meant we were able to donate an extra £400 to our charity.

Our Chinese friends in Singapore and Melbourne, where we stayed, in total, a week apiece, at either end of our cycle tour, gave us marvellous hospitality. They made us feel very much at home; and this was a great blessing to us, being so far away from England.

Chapter Seven

South Africa: 2012

This was the first time either of us had cycled in this beautiful country, with so much varied, magnificent scenery. We covered over 1,300 miles, exploring the Eastern and Western Cape Provinces, cycling from Cape Town to Port Elizabeth, along the coast and back again through the mountains and vineyards.

Jan had been to South Africa twice, over forty years ago, before the oppressive apartheid regime was abolished. What a difference this time! We now had the privilege of being able to mix freely with people from all the ethnic groups. Indeed, one of the highlights of our journey was worshipping in a Xhosa- speaking Church in an African township with our fellow Christians. This would have been nigh on impossible less than twenty years ago.

We arrived in Cape Town on 2nd. February, 2012 and cycled fifteen miles from the airport to the city centre, where we soon found suitable accommodation in a cheap hotel. In fact, everything was less expensive than in England. Most of the time we stayed in "Backpacker" hostels, youth hostels or reasonably priced self-catering accommodation. Many of these gave us substantial discounts, so we were able to donate the money saved to

"The Children's Society", the charity for which we did this trip.

We stayed in Cape Town three days, which gave us time to visit the city centre which is quite unique, with a magnificent view of Table Mountain in the background. Jan needed one of the gears on her bike fixed; we soon found a good bike shop and the job was done in no time at all. Indeed, Cape Town City Centre is surrounded by hills; so the gears were put to the test almost immediately!

During this time we were also able to adjust to the hot summer weather – a complete contrast to our cold mid-winter back home. We soon got used to it! We did a day's cycle ride around Cape Peninsula, which helped us to acclimatise. After obtaining some maps from the Tourist Information Centre, in the city, we were also able to plan our forthcoming trip.

Swimming in the Atlantic, from this part of the coast, was quite an experience: The water was as cold, if not colder, than our sea! However, it was very refreshing after a hard day's cycle ride and we soon warmed up in the hot sun afterwards.

We found an Anglican Church very near the hotel where we stayed and were given a very warm welcome. It was good to be able to worship together with white, black and coloured people. During the service the priest, an African, called us up to the front and prayed for a blessing upon us and safety for our journey, which encouraged us immensely.

Incidentally, the term "coloured" is used, in South Africa, to describe people of mixed race. It could be said that this ethnic group are truly indigenous to this country, having descended from inter-marriage between the early British white settlers and the native Hottentots, who were tribal Africans living in what is now known as Cape Province. Hence the name "Cape Coloureds" being used to identify these people. Those of European descent came from Britain and Holland a few hundred years ago, as did the "Bantu" Africans from Central and East Africa.

At the start of our journey, we cycled along the coast of the Western Cape, covering some of the ground we had cycled on our second day, in an easterly direction towards Cape Argulhas, which is the southernmost tip of the African continent. It was a wonderful experience for us when we actually arrived; and it was so windy that when we stopped to take a photo we were nearly blown off our bikes!

Once we left Cape Arghulas we were on the coast of the Indian Ocean, which was noticeably warmer than the Atlantic for swimming and also much less windy.

We were now on the way to Port Elizabeth, via the "Garden Route". Cycling over some of the hills could be very hard work at times; but the views we had were so spectacular, it was well worth the effort! In fact, we didn't even envy those who were sight-seeing by coach or car one bit! The scenery was truly amazing, with its vast bays and expanses of deep blue ocean.

A lot of our accommodation was run by white Afrikaans-speaking South Africans. These were people who, over 300 hundred years ago, came from Holland and consisted of mostly farmers who were able to develop the land; so that today it can yield a large variety of crops, fruit and vegetables, as well as support plenty of livestock. South Africa has quite a diverse climate, so nearly everything can be grown there.

We found these people extremely hospitable and very friendly. At one place the lady in charge of our accommodation cooked us a huge, typically South African breakfast, free of charge. This consisted of "mealie" porridge followed by "Boervors" (South African sausage), bacon, egg and tomato – a substantial meal for two hungry cyclists!

This lady was a semi-retired nurse and worked in the local African township, giving health education at the clinic there. One of her daughters was a midwife and she also worked in the township. The other daughter managed a hairdressing salon, on the premises of their large family house; and she employed a staff consisting of mostly black girls from the township.

When we first arrived in this town, called Joubertina, and enquired after a Church where we could worship on the Sunday, this same young woman suggested we go to the African Church in the township where, she said, we would enjoy a lively service. She even arranged for one of her staff to take us there! However, this young lady became ill over the weekend; but, not to let us down, she arranged for her pastor to collect us in his car!

We had a wonderful time that day: the warm fellowship with these African Christians was truly amazing! The Church, which consisted of a wooden shack, with a dry earthen floor and walls lined with newspaper, was packed to overflowing. Everyone was dressed in their "Sunday best" and all ages were represented. We looked quite scruffy in our shorts and T-shirts!

The young children were fascinated by us and especially with John's red beard, which they all took turns in stroking! It was quite an experience for this congregation to have two white English people with them; and it was a great privilege for us to be together in this way. This was, indeed, one of the highlights of our stay in South Africa.

As always, on our many cycling tours we trusted the Lord daily to provide for all our needs. We were certainly well-provided for in so many unexpected ways, despite the gruelling effort we had to put into our cycling. Indeed, the physical strength and stamina required was a miracle in itself.

We met an American couple of a similar age to ourselves at one hostel. They too were "independent travellers", using a hired car, not bicycles. Very kindly, they invited us to share their evening meal with them. This consisted of delicious steak, chips and salad, washed down with plenty of good South African red wine! For us this was a feast, as on our bikes we couldn't carry such provisions. Unless we stopped somewhere for a rest day, so we could do some shopping, our meals were very basic, although adequate and nutritious.

At another hostel a young "coloured" South African called Wayne invited us to share a meal with him on two successive nights. He was working in the area, supervising highway maintenance; and so he was living in the hostel for the duration of his appointment.

Wayne insisted on us joining him to eat, saying he didn't like cooking for himself alone! What an excellent cook he was too! The South African cuisine is superb, with a mix of the different cultures and ethnic groups of this country; namely, African, Dutch, English and a variety of Asian dishes as well.

As has already been mentioned, South Africa supports a wide diversity of home-grown produce and is almost self-sufficient. The only commodity it lacks is oil. It is otherwise potentially a rich country with coal, gold and diamonds in good supply.

There was another hostel, which we discovered just before it was dark, after our longest cycle ride of the whole trip. It was also very arduous, with several mountains along our route. Not only this, Jan had a heavy cold which didn't help matters. This in itself was quite unusual, as she hadn't had a cold for at least two years! John had already had a cold a few days previous; but this was on a rest day, so he was able to take it easy!

However, we were given a very warm welcome at this hostel and we soon settled in. It was managed by two young African men: one was of the Xhosa tribe and came from East London, further up the coast from Port Elizabeth; and the other came from Malawi, in Central Africa. This country is situated north of Mozambique and is adjacent to Zambia, where Jan spent two years as a V.S.O. from 1968 to 1970. They were both Christians and it was a joy to meet them. We were even given a substantial cooked breakfast, early the next morning so we could get a good start to the day.

It was a wonderful experience, for us both, to be able to mix freely with these Africans on an equal level – something unheard of just a few years ago.

In one of the backpacker hostels where we stayed, we met an African pastor from a church in a township in Pretoria. He had travelled south to help his son move house. The pastor was roughly in the same age group as us and it was interesting to hear about the struggles the Africans had experienced during the apartheid era and how this pastor had received such tremendous support from his white Christian brothers and sisters in the Church. Jan, in particular, was able to share her experiences of visiting South Africa in 1969, when on leave from her work in the African Bush of Western Zambia; and in 1970, when travelling down to Cape Town, to return to England on a passenger boat. They had both suffered from apartheid in different ways; and now they could strike up a genuine friendship.

The pastor had two young men from his church with him and we had a great time of fellowship, as we talked and shared our faith together. In fact, we discovered a very strong Christian presence in South Africa wherever we went. This, we believe, has been this country's saving grace; for there is no doubt that without it democracy would have only happened as a result of a huge bloodshed and a tremendous loss of life. We can thank God for the Church, political leaders and the people of South Africa, who were instrumental in bringing this about.

On four of the Sundays we were in South Africa, we worshipped at local Anglican Churches, where we met many English speaking white South Africans, some of whom gave generous donations to our charity. The majority of these people were retired and a good few had been missionary nurses from England, who had now made their permanent home in South Africa.

The first and last Sunday of our stay we worshipped at St. James' Church in Seapoint, Cape Town. The vicar, an African, prayed for us on both occasions and asked us to convey their greetings to the people of our own Church of St. James in Poolstock, Wigan. This, of course we did on returning home.

One Sunday we went to an Afrikaans speaking Church in Barrydale, in the Western Cape Province. We had been unable to find the local English speaking Church and discovered this Dutch Reformed Church quite by accident; but it turned out to be God's provision for us: The whole service was conducted in Afrikaans, which could be described as a "bastard" Dutch language. Needless to say, we didn't understand a word! The Minister conducting the service understandably probably thought we were Afrikaaners!

During the service several hymns were sung, whose tunes were familiar to us; however, we couldn't always remember the words! At one point all the men were asked to stand up; so John did as he was told! The minister prayed very fervently for these men, only in Afrikaans, so we were none the wiser! However, at the end of the service we were told that the prayer had been for a special blessing upon the men and their wives and families; and that they would bear the fruits of the Holy Spirit in their lives. We were both very blessed, when this was explained to us later on.

At the end of the service we were invited to join the rest of the congregation for tea and biscuits. We were made very welcome, especially when they learned we were from England. Communication at this stage wasn't a problem, as most white South Africans are bilingual and, therefore speak both Afrikaans and English fluently, although, usually one or other of them is their "mother" tongue.

It was here that we met a wonderful lady called Maggi. She prayed for us (in English) a very heartfelt and inspired prayer, that our marriage would be blessed, we would continue to walk with the Lord and serve Him faithfully. We were very moved by the genuine love she showed us. Then just as we were about to depart, after hugging each other "goodbye", Maggi called us back and invited us to go with her to meet a fellow cyclist, who lived nearby.

Maggi had already told us she was ninety-four years old, although we found this hard to believe: her mind was sharp, she was slim, smartly dressed and she even drove her own car! So off we all went to meet Dave, the cyclist, and his wife, Cathy.

Shortly, we arrived at their house and straight away, we were made very welcome. Cathy even prepared a large plate of sandwiches and a pot of tea, almost immediately. As was our experience throughout our journey, we found the South Africans to be a very hospitable people. Jan also had the same experience over forty years ago.

Dave was of English origin, born in South Africa; and Cathy was from a farming family in Zimbabwe. We discovered Dave led cycle tours in the Cape Province; and he was able to give us some useful tips to enable us to complete our journey back to Cape Town, on a scenic, less busy route. We were very grateful for his advice and, what is more, we were able to follow his directions without getting lost!

After our visit Maggi took us back to her home – a delightful little bungalow, specially built for senior citizens. She gave us both a cool drink and showed us around, including her pretty, well-kept garden, where we took some photos of each other. These we will always treasure. Later on that afternoon, Dave called to take us to swim in a river, situated in a mountain pass, amidst the most beautiful scenery either of us had ever seen. It was sheer bliss to be able to bathe in the cool water, under a waterfall and ease our aching limbs! This was another highlight of our journey in this beautiful country.

We arrived back in Cape Town after four weeks of hard cycling. The last day, as we cycled along the coast of Western Cape, was the hardest of all, because we had to battle against a strong head-wind for over sixty miles. It was quite exhausting; but our determination to complete this last leg of our journey kept us going.

Along the way we were able to see a view of Robben Island, where Nelson Mandela was imprisoned for twenty-eight years. It was hard to believe that this was in our own lifetime; we could even remember him going into prison! And since his release in 1991 (the year we were married), not only had apartheid been abolished; but Nelson Mandela himself became South Africa's first black President in 1994!

When we finally reached Cape Town, early that evening, we spent considerable time searching for suitable accommodation. We cycled around the districts of Green Point and Sea Point, where we had previously stayed and where there was an abundance of budget hostels, to no avail. A major long-distance cycling event was taking place the next day; and everywhere was booked up.

After at least two hours we found an International Youth Hostel, which was completely full save for one single room! We persuaded the Manager to let us stay; and she "bent" the rules and allowed us to have the room for the night. In this hostel were many cyclists who had come to take part in the big event, which was 1000km (62.5 miles) around the Cape Peninsula. When we met them at breakfast the next day they, naturally, thought we were also taking part. We told them that we had already cycled over one thousand miles (1600km) during the past four weeks and that we had completed our journey. They were not only amazed; but agreed we now deserved a rest!

After breakfast we made our way to St. James' Church, in Sea Point, about three miles away; and, along our route, we were able to see the start of the "Argus", which is what this annual bike event was called. It was quite exciting to watch; but, for once, we were glad we weren't taking part!

We arrived in good time for the morning worship at St. James' and were welcomed back after our long trip. The priest remembered us well, called us to the front and gave thanks to God for our safe return. It was good to be back amongst friends; and we were able to thank them for their prayers.

We now had three days to "recover", before flying back to Manchester; but first we had to find accommodation. We soon discovered some self-catering apartments in Green Point, very close to a beautiful park and Cape Town's famous "Waterfront", both of which we now had the time to explore – on foot.

On making enquiries at the "Waterfront Apartments", we were told that if we came back in an hour's time there would something suitable available for us. This was to give the present occupants time to check out, as they had come to watch the cycling event, which lasted until the early evening. Whilst waiting we went to watch some more ourselves:

Not only was it of great interest to us as cyclists, it was also good to see participants representing all of South Africa's ethnic groups. Just a few years ago such an event would have only been open to white people. There were other cyclists who were also spectators; and we joined in cheering on these brave cyclists. We knew their course was a gruelling one, having done part of it ourselves.

When we returned to the Waterfront Apartments our rooms had been made ready. We were delighted with our accommodation. It was very spacious, with a large balcony which enabled us to sit outside which was especially welcome in the warm climate of this part of the world. It was also let at a reasonable price. In fact, we were given a discount, which we were able to donate to the N.S.P.C.C. – the charity for which we did this bike ride.

We spent the next three days relaxing in the large park opposite where we stayed and exploring Cape Town's magnificent waterfront, as well as parts of the city we hadn't already seen, including its beautiful cathedral. We also spent time swimming in the Atlantic Ocean; and, when the tide was out, in the open-air swimming pool, both of which were very close by.

However, the highlight was when we climbed to the top of the "Lion's Head". We had promised ourselves, before we set off on our cycle tour, that, when we returned to Cape Town, we would climb Table Mountain. Jan had wanted to do this back in 1970, before she sailed home to England; but she had to be satisfied with reaching the summit in a cable car! This was due to lack of time and the fact that she was with a friend, who was expecting a baby within a few days!

In March 2012, we left the Waterfront Apartments with a view to climbing Table Mountain; and walked for several miles before arriving at the foothills of this magnificent group of mountains. When we reached the point where we would have to decide whether to continue on to Table

Mountain or go towards Lion's Head, we realised that we could never make it to the summit before dark. In order to climb Table Mountain, we should have taken a bus to where the ascent began; but we didn't realise just how far away it was when we set off! A mountain of this size looks a lot nearer than it actually is!

We were, at first, disappointed; but then realised that we could manage to climb the Lion's Head and still be home in time for tea! It was a clear, sunny day and we still had several hours of daylight left; so we set of to climb this very high peak, next door to Table Mountain. We were really rewarded with some wonderful views from the top; and any previous reservations we may have had about our decision were vanquished! It wasn't an easy climb by any means and there were some "tricky" moments, especially on the sheer parts of the peak, where hand rails were provided; but we made it!

The descent was quite difficult to start with; but after the hard bit it was just a very long, downhill walk to the bottom and then, a few miles back to where we were staying. We were very pleased with what we had been able to accomplish and thanked God for our safe return. Needless to say, we slept soundly that night!

Our cycle tour in South Africa was a trip of a lifetime and we have some unforgettable memories to treasure for the rest of our lives. We thank God, from the bottom of our hearts, for all the people who prayed for us, that we able to do this journey and arrive home safe and sound.

Chapter Eight

North America: 2013

On 2nd September 2013, we set off to fly from Manchester, via London, to Vancouver in British Columbia, Canada. Our intention was to cycle to San Diego, approximately 1,900 miles away. This included all of the West Coast of the United States of America, as well as part of the coast of British Columbia. We would be travelling through the States of Washington, Oregon and California, reaching the Mexican border at the end of our journey.

As always, we did feel a little apprehensive, not knowing exactly what lay ahead of us, only that we would travel through some stunning scenery - so we had been told. Incidentally, the people who had tales to tell regarding visiting this part of the world had travelled in luxury, either by car or on a cruise!

It was, perhaps just as well we didn't know what to expect, as it turned out to be the hardest and hilliest cycle tour we have ever done! And, with the exception of Malaysia and Thailand in 2007, which for the most part was fairly flat, it was the longest. There were many very steep climbs for most of the way; and it was a long journey.

However, we were strengthened in knowing that many folk were praying for us, both back home, in America and even in Singapore and India. Friends, neighbours, our local church and the staff and pupils of St. James' Primary School, Wigan, people in Canada and the U.S.A. whom we'd recently met and Christians in Asia, whom we'd encountered on previous cycle tours, were all praying for our safety and well-being throughout our journey. The Christians we have met over the years have become our life-long friends; and we know we can count upon them to pray for us. This is a great joy and blessing.

One of our Chinese friends in Singapore had even contacted an old school friend in Vancouver, asking him to assist us on our arrival in Canada. This person, although unable to accommodate us, owing to a pre-arranged holiday with his wife, got in touch with a friend who was a retired pastor, who also lived in Vancouver and asked if he could help in any way possible.

Thank God for the internet! Our friend, Ming in Singapore vouched for our characters and integrity (bless him) and the Reverend David in Vancouver e-mailed us and arrangements were made:

Dave met us at the Airport, with a vehicle large enough for both our bikes, and took us to his home, where we were greeted warmly by his wife Beth and made very welcome. Dave and Beth originally came from England – Dave from Islington, London and Beth from Bingley in Yorkshire. We felt at home with them immediately and thanked God for His provision of these kind people.

We spent two days in Vancouver and Dave took us out in his car and showed us as much as he could of this beautiful city. Beth was still working; so Dave was free and he looked after us very well.

On the day we departed from their home, Beth had to arise at the crack of dawn and drive Dave to the Airport for him to fly to California to a Christian pastors' convention.

This meant we had to see ourselves off and lock the house. What a privilege to be trusted in this way!

Our stay with Beth and Dave was a wonderful provision from our Lord, who promises us that He "will go before you and will be with you" (Deuteronomy 31:8).

We needed physical strength and moral courage as well as sheer determination to do what we did; and we can truly thank God for supplying all our needs, including a bed for each night and food for the journey each day.

There were times when we were tempted to despair; but our faith was often miraculously rewarded as we hoped and trusted the Lord.

On one occasion we had cycled nearly seventy miles in Washington State; and it was beginning to get dark. We saw what we thought was a motel; but it turned out to be a private bungalow, rented by two American couples, having a few days' holiday! They too were relative strangers to this part of the world, coming as they did from the New England States, on the East Coast; and they were sympathetic with our predicament.

We were welcomed with open arms, given a refreshing drink of cold beer and invited to spend the night in one of the spare rooms. This was very spacious, as was the large kitchen made available for our use; so we were very comfortable indeed.

We were given huge bath towels and thoroughly enjoyed a hot shower, before eating a light meal and then, later on, retiring to bed. Needless to say, we slept very well, as we always did after a hard day's cycling.

Another time, again it was dark, we were quite weary at the end of a long day's cycling and we hadn't seen any signs of human habitation for several miles. We had been travelling through one of Oregon's large National Parks when suddenly we saw a wooden shack with the American flag flying from its roof!

We knocked on the door and were greeted by a Native American, well over six feet tall. He was a Red Indian of the Quinault tribe; and he kindly invited us to stay the night. His name was Dean and, first, he offered us the use of his tent; but we asked if he was able to accommodate us under his roof, for which we would pay him. He then kindly gave us floor space, a mattress and blankets, in a separate area from his own, which we gladly accepted.

However, had we seen the state of Dean's home we might have had second thoughts! It consisted of one large room, the kitchen area, which was none too clean, the main area, strewn with clothes and all sorts of things and a curtained-off space, where Dean had his bed and T.V. There was also a shower and toilet with a small hand basin, along a narrow passage: The least said about these the better! There was no electricity and only cold water.

We were still grateful; and thanked God for His provision, remembering that our Lord, Himself was born in a smelly, dirty stable!

Dean set a couple of mousetraps before we went to bed. It was just as well, because we did have a few encounters with members of the rodent family during the night; though there were none in the traps by the next morning!

After a basic breakfast of bread and jam early the next day, we were ready to get on our way. We said "goodbye" to Dean, who was still in bed, watching T.V. We presume he had slept, as he was engaged in the same occupation as when we had said "goodnight" to him the day before! We thanked him and promised to pray for him, for which, as well as the money we gave him, he seemed grateful.

Needless to say, Dean wasn't living the lifestyle of his ancestors and was probably very lonely. His home was previously owned by his grandparents who had died, after which Dean moved in. And his mother lived about five miles away, with whom Dean had a hot meal each day. We encouraged Dean to join a local Indian Christian Fellowship, as once his grandparents did; and he did express some interest. We can only hope that he took our advice!

It took us exactly five weeks to do the whole trip, including a "rest day" each week, which we always took after six consecutive days of cycling. We were usually quite exhausted by the time we stopped; and we needed these days to gather strength for the next stage of our journey.

We found it quite incredible that we actually cycled 1,900 miles from British Columbia through the states of Washington, Oregon and California to our final destination in San Diego, near the Mexican border. The people we met on our journey found it hard to believe too! We were able to tell them, quite frankly, that God had given us the strength; and we were certainly convinced of this.

We cycled through vast areas of forest, mountain lakes, along the spectacular coastline of the Pacific Ocean and through the cities of San Francisco and Los Angeles. We experienced some magnificent views at the top of each climb, which made our efforts so worthwhile and gave us a tremendous sense of achievement when we finally reached San Diego, at the end of our journey.

When we approached San Francisco's famous Golden Gate, a mist came down over the Bay and the visibility was very poor. At first we were very disappointed; but, just as we were clear of the bridge, the sky cleared and we were able to see a splendid view of the city, surrounded by a vast area of deep blue water. We were able to take some good photos before continuing our journey to Foster City, on the far side of the Bay.

Here we stayed two nights with Cheryl (Ming's daughter from Singapore), her husband, Leon and their little girl, Noella, aged twenty-one months. They looked after us very well and sent us on our way, rested and replenished by their excellent Chinese cuisine.

Four hundred miles before we reached our final destination - about a week's cycling, we were desperately trying to find somewhere to spend the night. It was weekend and the coastal resort of Cambria was "invaded" by people coming from many miles inland in search of the sand, sea and sun. We tried the youth hostel in vain; but they did phone and book the only room available in the town, in a nearby motel, where we could spend the night. After eating a light meal we "fell" into bed and were soon soundly asleep.

It has to be explained that every night, with the exception of five when having a rest day and, therefore, staying two nights, we slept in a different bed, in a strange room. The beds varied from twins, which were each the size of a small double bed (so we only needed one!), standard size (about five feet wide!) and king-size (about six feet plus wide!) Neither of us are very big; so we were quite lost in a king-size bed, which could have quite easily have accommodated two more adults of our size!

The night we stayed in the aforementioned motel, it was spent in a room with a standard double bed and cluttered with over–large furniture. Jan got up in the middle of the night to pay a call to nature and, on her return, misjudged the width and fell between the bed and the bedside locker! Unfortunately, she broke the knuckle on her right hand; but this was only diagnosed three weeks later, on returning home and visiting Wigan Infirmary's Accident and Emergency Department! So, convincing herself it was only a bad sprain, she continued to cycle undeterred (although, she had her doubts) for the remainder of the journey!

Sheer determination, faith and adrenaline kept Jan going! Fortunately, there were no more accidents; but we did forget our one and only change of clothing at the youth hostel in Monterey. This consisted of a pair of shorts each, T-shirts and underwear.

On arriving at the next hostel, which was at San Luis Obispo, we told one of the voluntary workers our predicament and he very kindly phoned the hostel at Monterey and asked them to post our clothes to the next hostel, where we planned to be within the next two days.

This young man's name was Patrick, who came from Fulham in London; so he and Jan had a lot in common, Jan also coming from Fulham. They were able to share many memories of their home town and how it had changed over the years. Patrick had also cycled part of the same route as us, with a group of friends. However, when he reached San Luis Obispo Patrick decided to "call it a day"; and he offered his services as a volunteer, at the youth hostel. Quite honestly, we didn't blame him!

When we arrived at Santa Barbara, two days later, our clothes hadn't arrived. Apparently, they had been sent to the wrong hostel! By this time we were considering buying ourselves replacements, if we could find any reasonably-priced clothing (California is very expensive); and the time to shop. It hardly seemed worth the effort as we were now on the last leg of our journey. However, our clothes miraculously arrived early the next morning, just before we departed! This was certainly an answer to our fervent prayers and, needless to say, we were very pleased!

We continued our journey towards our destination, through South California, along hundreds of miles of beautiful coastline, via Santa Monica and Los Angeles. In order to avoid the highways, which, for the most part are prohibited to cyclists, we had to cycle through Pendleton Camp, a training centre and base for the American Marines. This meant that we were required to produce our passports on entering the camp. Thereafter we had no trouble cycling through this, mainly traffic-free area. We soon found our coastal road on exiting the camp; and continued towards San Diego.

On the last day of our tour we somehow "lost" the coastal road, which cyclists could use; and we found ourselves on the "highway"! It was really quite safe, with an inside lane similar to the "hard shoulder" on our motorways. However, strictly speaking, we weren't supposed to be there!

We travelled on until it started to become dark; and then considered our best option was to come off the highway and find our way to the youth hostel in San Diego. Once off the highway it was extremely difficult to know which road to take; and the fact that it was early evening and already quite dark didn't help. We waited a few minutes in order to ask a driver passing by which direction we should take; and, very soon, a kind young man called Mohammed, from the Middle East, stopped to help us.

Mohammed didn't recommend that we cycled the next fifteen miles in the dark, as he feared we'd find the route very difficult to navigate at this time of the day. However, he wouldn't leave us until he could get help. Unfortunately, his car was too small for us plus our bikes; otherwise he would have taken us himself. So he tried to contact one or two of his friends, with larger vehicles, to come and collect us.

In the meantime, before Mohammed had any response, a young couple, with a roof-rack on their car stopped to assist. It turned out that the driver, Robert, was a keen cyclist with his own workshop, and his fiancée, Mara, also cycled. They took no time in leading us to a safe lay-by, with Mohammed behind us in his car, to protect us!

Robert then placed our bikes securely on the roof-rack and we were taken to the youth hostel in San Diego. These people were definitely "Angels", sent by the Lord. We had no doubt about this!

Once we had settled into the youth hostel, where we were very comfortable, with a large room to ourselves, we could now look forward to a week of rest and relaxation, before cycling to the airport ten miles away and returning home. This was to be a short holiday for us both and we were able to restore ourselves.

The weather, as nearly always in this part of South California, was warm and pleasant. We spent most of our time relaxing in the sun, on the nearby beach and swimming in the sea. We also borrowed some body-boards from the hostel and did a bit of surfing.

On two occasions we "treated" ourselves to a "short" bike ride! On the first we cycled a round trip of twenty-five miles and explored "Mission Bay". This included a visit to a different beach and a swim in the sea. The other cycle ride took us to the end of the Peninsula, known as Point Loma, where the Naval Base is situated. This was an uphill climb all the way; and we had some magnificent views from the top. It was well worth the effort.

We also visited an Episcopal Church, near to the Youth Hostel, where we were able to attend a mid-week Holy Communion as well as the Sunday Worship Service. Both times we were made very welcome. Some of the congregation came from England and Ireland; and they had retired to live here. They were particularly pleased to meet us and, on the Sunday, the Irish lady gave us a loaf of home-made bread. It was very tasty!

Talking about food – everyday, at breakfast, a pancake mix was prepared by one of the youth hostel staff and a large griddle pan placed on the gas stove to heat up. We would always be the first down to breakfast at 7am and cooked for ourselves a "few" delicious pancakes, laden with maple syrup! They were irresistible! We found it hard to believe just how hungry we were; we had become "shadows" of our former selves, after cycling 1,900 miles over the past five weeks!

One day, when returning to the hostel, after a day on the beach, we were told by the manager that Robert and Mara had phoned and wanted to take us out for an evening meal. We soon arranged this for the following day; and we were taken to a nearby Mexican restaurant for a traditional vegetarian dish, which was quite delicious. We also sampled some good, locally-brewed San Diego beer, which went down very well! While we were there we were "serenaded" by a Mexican guitarist, singing "Guantanamera"! It was very romantic and we all relaxed and enjoyed ourselves.

Later we were taken, by car, to "Downtown" San Diego, to an Italian ice cream parlour, for our final course. We were just about able to manage this too! It was a lovely evening and we shall never forget the genuine friendship and kind hospitality given to us by Robert and Mara. We pray that God will bless their marriage and their life together.

We also made friends with two young men from the East, one from Korea, Sean, and the other from Japan, Noah. They were staying at the same hostel and Sean had already met us cycling several miles back, a few days before arriving in San Diego. Sean had cycled a similar route, starting from Los Angeles; so we had a lot in common with him. Both these young men showed us tremendous respect and treated us as if we were their parents! We grew quite fond of them and they became, temporarily, our adopted sons. Sean was particularly helpful to Jan in allowing her to use his iPad, in order for her to send e-mails back to England and to people we had met in America, on our journey.

We were together the whole week; and we all left on the same day, to travel to our respective homes. It was a nostalgic moment for us, as we hugged one another and said "goodbye". Reluctantly, we said farewell to our new friends and the staff at the hostel, whom we had also got to know quite well.

We left San Diego on October 21st 2013 to travel back home to Wigan, with many happy memories of our trip, the scenery and the people we met.

Chapter Nine

"Three Score Years and Ten... And Back in the Saddle Again"

Our last major cycle tour overseas, was in North America in the late summer and early autumn of 2013. Since then, in the spring of 2014, we did a "small" tour (570 miles) in the Midlands and South of England. This we named "A Pilgrimage Cathedral Tour" which we used to raise money for the repair of our church roof, from which the lead had been stolen.

However, we did plan and, indeed, booked the flights for a tour in Venezuela, South America, for which we should have departed on 28th October, returning seven weeks later on 16th December 2014. This would have included celebrating Jan's 70th birthday on 9th December.

A few months beforehand John had asked Jan how she would like to celebrate this special birthday, whether she wanted a relaxing, lazy holiday somewhere in the sun (staying in one place!) or "an adventure". Needless to say, she chose the latter!

We planned to cycle along the coast from Caracas, the capital, for as long as we had time; and then, on our return, stop over on the Island of San Margarita to celebrate Jan's birthday and spend a few days exploring the island on our bikes. However, this was not to be!

We have a camper van, in which we spend the summer months staying in some of our favourite places in North Wales and the Peak District, where we pursue what we enjoy most – being outdoors walking, cycling and swimming in the sea. Over the years we have made friends with many folk at the local churches, as well as on the campsites. Thus, we are very much "at home", whenever we go away.

In late September, whilst staying at a campsite on the border of the "Staffordshire Moorlands" and the "Derbyshire Dales", in the Peak District, Jan had a serious accident on her bicycle.

The weather was warm and sunny; we had cycled along the "Tissington Trail", which is a disused railway line; and we had exited at the Buxton/Ashbourne Road, where we began our descent over the moors on a quiet country lane towards Thorpe – a small village in the Dove Valley.

Without any warning, Jan's cycle went into a skid on the loose gravel in the middle of the road. She hit the ground very hard and was unable to get up. This was not surprising because, as it turned out, she had broken her left elbow and forearm, as well as her left hip!

Reluctantly, John had to leave Jan at the side of the road, while he cycled down to the village a mile away. There the owner of the garage phoned for an ambulance, put John's bike in a secure place and then took him back in his car to where Jan was. He then picked Jan's bike up and took it back to be kept safe with John's. Incidentally, Jan's bicycle was undamaged!

Our bikes were later collected by Peter, the owner of the campsite where we were staying, and he kept them in his garage until we were ready to return home. We can't thank these people enough for their kindness towards us.

In the meantime, four walkers – two ladies with their dogs and a young couple who were out walking were looking after Jan, and, even when John had arrived, they stayed with her until the ambulance came.

Jan was very well looked after by the paramedics, who gave her morphine and took her to the Royal Derby Hospital, where she was admitted for nine days and also given excellent care, following two major operations performed the next day.

The first was to insert a metal plate and pins to the elbow and forearm, which was broken in three places, followed by a total hip replacement due to the neck of the femur being too badly damaged to do otherwise. Jan was under a general anaesthetic for a few hours! She hadn't a clue what had been done till much later on!

John stayed at the campsite until Jan was discharged, given plenty of support by the owners of the campsite (Peter and Janette) and food each day at the hospital, where he visited Jan daily, using three buses to do the journey. He cycled the first day, covering sixty miles, on a very hilly ride!

Jan was discharged home at the beginning of October and referred to Wrightington Hospital for the care of her hip, Wigan Infirmary for her arm as well as her G.P. and both Hospital and Community Physiotherapy Departments. She has nothing but praise for all the health professionals involved, the excellent care they have given and the encouragement she has received from them all.

Jan was told she could swim in eight weeks' time; and she would be able to cycle within three months from the date of the operations. She dispensed with her crutch almost immediately, using it only for walks of over five miles. She actually walked to Wrightington Hospital for her first outpatient appointment (seven miles on country footpaths) and was told by the Doctor not to "overdo it"! This was only seven weeks after her operation!

She persevered with swimming until, on Christmas Eve she managed to swim a mile. And, on Christmas Day, she got on her bike for the first time. It was one of the best Christmas presents she has ever had!

Apart from when there has been frost and ice around, Jan has cycled regularly ever since. She has also continued to swim a mile four times a week, except when she had to have a second operation on her left arm at the end of January, necessitating two weeks off. But she is now back in the saddle again!

It has to be said that we believe this to be a miracle and we truly praise the Lord for His healing. Many people have prayed for Jan over the past few months – our church, the local primary school and Christian friends, at home and abroad. We thank them for their faith and pray for God's blessings upon them all.

We haven't yet planned another overseas cycle tour; but we are giving it serious consideration. So watch this space!

Appendix

Cycling Clothing, Food and Equipment Required for a Six Week Tour: -

1. Temperate Climate in the Summer Season
I.e. New Zealand, Australia and North America
Clothing: -

Cycling Shorts;
Long Cycling Pants;
Thermal Vest;
Cycling Short-Sleeved Shirt;
Cycling Long-Sleeved Shirt;
Short Cycling Socks;
Long Woollen Socks;
Underwear;
Warm Cycling Gloves;
Cycling Mitts;
Cotton Cap;
Woolly Cap;
Woolly Mitts;
2 Handkerchiefs;
Lightweight Shorts;
Lightweight Fleece Top;
Cotton T- Shirt;
Waterproof Cycling Jacket;
Cycling Jacket;
Cycling Helmet;
Summer Cycling Shoes;
Walking Sandals;
Swimming Costume, Trunks and Goggles.

2. Tropical Climate
I.e. Malaysia, Thailand, Singapore and India

Cycling Shorts;
Cycling Shirt;
Underwear;
Two Handkerchiefs;
Medium Length Shorts;
T-Shirt;
Running Shorts;
Running Vest;
African- Print "Sarong";
Cotton Cap;
Sunhat;
Walking Sandals;
Cycling Sandals;
Cycling Helmet;
Cycling Mitts;
Swimming Costume, Trunks and Goggles.

3. Mediterranean Climate; i.e. South Africa

The same as for a tropical climate.
N.B. All the articles of clothing listed, relate to one item of each per person.

Toilet Articles: -

Toothbrush and Toothpaste;

Comb;

Flannel;

Sports Chamois;

White Petroleum Jelly (225gm.);

Sunblock Stick;

Strong Sunscreen (30-40);

1 Large Bar Green Soap.

Luggage Items: -

4 Waterproof Pannier Bags;

2 Small Rucksacks;

One Money Belt Each;

One Wallet and One Purse;

Two Bungee Straps Each.

Food Items: -

Tea Bags x 80;

200g. Jar Coffee (in plastic container);

500g. Instant Drinking Chocolate (in plastic bottle);

1 Jar Clear Honey (for porridge);

1 Jar each of Set Honey; Peanut Butter; Chocolate Spread and Lemon Curd;

2lb. Porridge Oats;

Salt; Pepper and Chili (in small plastic containers).

Sundry Items: -

1 Penknife each;

Small pair Scissors; Nail File and Clippers;

1 Pair Reading Glasses each;

1 Pair Sunglasses each;

Elastoplast Strip; Analgesic and Anti-inflammatory Tablets;

GMPTE Bus/Train Passes;

Credit Card;

1 Wristwatch each;

2 Ball-point Pens;

Diary and Address Book;

Camera; Battery Charger and Adaptor;

Passports and Travel Documents;

Travel Insurance Details;

Holy Bible and Study Notes;

2 Small Vacuum Flasks;

1 Butter Knife; 2 Teaspoons; 1 Small Serrated Knife; 1 Tin Opener and 1 Tea Towel.

Bicycle Equipment: -

6 Spare Inner Tubes;

1 Bicycle Pump each;

Tyre Levers and Tools;

1 Large Combination Lock;

2 Water Bottles each;

Bicycle Computers.